TWENTY YEARS AT THE STADIUM OF LIGHT

Written by Rob Mason

A TWOCAN PUBLICATION

©2017. Published by twocan under licence from Sunderland AFC.

ISBN 978-1-911502-59-3

PICTURE CREDITS: Action Images, Getty Images, Mirrorpix, Press Association, Rob Mason, Sunderland AFC.

ACKNOWLEDGEMENT: Barry Jackson for page 144 statistics.

STADIUM OF LIGHT

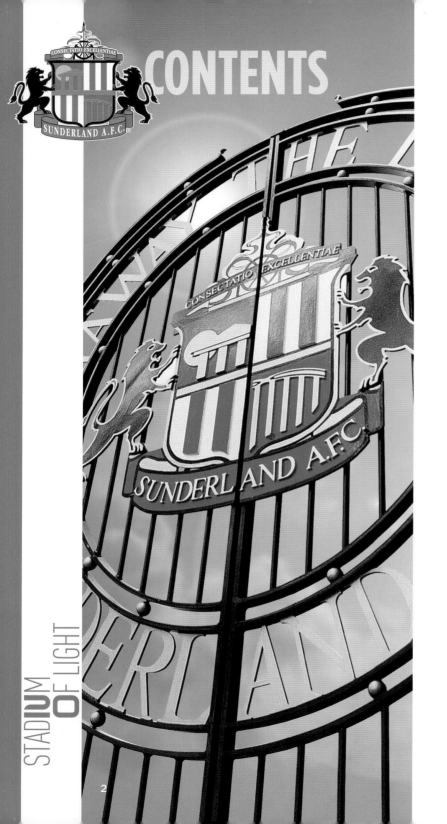

CONTENTS

STADIUM OF LIGHT

As the Stadium of Light reaches its 20th anniversary, it now has a history of its own. Wonderful memories include the opening night against Ajax, the 105-point team with Kevin Phillips and Niall Quinn, my own personal favourite match - the Play-Off thriller against Sheffield United in 1998 and home-grown players such as Jordan Henderson and Jordan Pickford coming from the Academy of Light to the Stadium of Light.

And on the international scene. England have been pleased to stage three full internationals at the Stadium of Light, the most recent in 2016. That's as many times as England played full internationals at Roker Park in its entire 99 years.

Already the club have spent longer at the Stadium of Light than the combined total of all six of the places they used for home games before moving to Roker Park. The Stadium of Light will be the club's home for many more decades to come. It is not just a football ground where Sunderland stage their home fixtures, it is a home from home for all supporters.

Just as at Roker Park where, like me, many of you knew your forefathers had roared on the Lads, so now at the Stadium of Light, new generations are coming forward to take the club on into the rest of the century. Those of us who have seen the first 20 years at the Stadium of Light are in turn the forefathers of the supporters of the present and future. The Stadium of Light is a home fit for the people we want to pass our legacy on to. It is a world away from Roker Park which had been neglected for decades before we said farewell.

As the longest-serving chairman in the club's history, it was my responsibility to equip the club for the 21st century. Making sure Sunderland AFC did not remain in a much loved, but ageing museum piece of a football ground with a decreasing capacity, was the task we were faced with as the new millennium approached. We look now at some big clubs in out-dated stadiums and know we did the right thing in creating what was the biggest and best new football ground built in England in the second half of the 20th century.

It still remains my dream that at sometime in the future the Stadium of Light will be even bigger. After just three seasons we had to extend the ground and when the stadium was constructed, we did it in such a way to future-proof it for the long term. In time, and with the right success, the remainder can be extended just as the North Stand was, so that eventually the capacity can rise to an awesome 66,000.

For that to happen we have to keep the faith, just as I kept the faith when people were asking why I wanted to build a ground that was so big when our crowds were under half of the initial capacity we created. I knew what Sunderland was capable of. I still do. That's why I am so proud that the very special people who make Sunderland the most special of clubs have a home from home that is first class. In time we hope to see an equally top-class team to grace it and lead to it being extended further.

FOREWORD

Supporting Sunderland is about family and friends as well as football. They are entwined together with a pride in who we are and where we're from. The Stadium of Light is a home we can be proud of. It is for us all.

Sir Bob Murray CBE

FOR US ALL

3

The Stadium of Light was the biggest football ground built in the country in the second half of the twentieth century, but it wasn't big enough for Sunderland. The initial 42,000 capacity quickly proved insufficient, as in the early seasons of the SoL, Sunderland played magical football under Peter Reid, with Niall Quinn and SuperKev to the fore.

After just three seasons, the north stand had to be extended, increasing the capacity to just under 49,000. Chairman Bob Murray was the visionary. Steeped in red and white, Bob was a life-time supporter and knew that if Sunderland did well there was phenomenal support to draw from. With that knowledge and belief, Murray and vice-chairman John Fickling had ensured that when the stadium was built, it was constructed in such a manner that future expansion was 'built-in'. Consequently, when 42,000 seats evidently were too few, the process in lifting the roof of the north stand, extending the Premier Concourse around behind the goal, and putting a roof back on was relatively simple stuff.

Moreover, should Sunderland ever reach the levels supporters have always dreamed of; the successes previous generations of Sunderland supporters enjoyed, then the Stadium of Light has the ability to be further developed, with the south and east stands also easy in construction terms to expand. A final capacity in the region of 66,000 is possible. Accepted as a 'Host City' in England's bids for the 2018 and 2006 FIFA World Cups, in 2006 Sunderland was destined to be a semi-final ground in which case that 66,000 capacity may have been reached within the opening decade.

If you were ten when you were at the opening game at the Stadium of Light against Ajax you would be 30 as the SoL celebrates its 20th anniversary. A generation of fans already exist who have only known the Stadium of Light as Sunderland's home. In contrast, if you had been ten and had seen Sunderland's earliest activities in 1879 or the first recorded game in 1880, by the time you had reached 30 you could have seen Sunderland play at seven home grounds! These days, each of these is marked with a blue plaque signifying that Sunderland once played there.

Starting at The Blue House Field in Hendon, the club staged matches at a field near The Cedars, moved on to where the Ashbrooke Sports Club now stands, then crossed the river to play at 'The Dolly Field' near the Wolsey pub. From there they moved to Abbs Field near the top of Side Cliffe Road in Fulwell, on to Newcastle Road and then in 1898 to Roker Park.

As the 20th anniversary of The Stadium of Light is celebrated in 2017, it is worth noting that already it has been the club's home for longer than the first six of the club's homes combined. Having called Roker Park home for 99 years, clearly Roker Park remains in a sense the club's traditional home, but the Stadium of Light already has its own history and that history will keep growing.

The League Championship has been won in 1999, 2005 and 2007, in 1999 with a record 105 points. England have staged full internationals at the Stadium of Light in 1999, 2003 and 2016. Other representative games staged at the ground include England games at U21, U20 and U16 levels as well as the final and a quarter-final of the European U16 Championships, plus national cup finals including the English Schools' FA Premier League U14s and FA Carlsberg Sunday Cup.

As Simon Grayson was appointed manager for the start of the 2017-18 campaign, he became the 14th manager (excluding 'caretakers') to have taken the hot-seat at the Stadium of Light. Can you think of them all? The pages to come will bring back a few memories - some better than others.

Supporters in the Stadium of Light era have had a new generation of heroes to cheer. From Kevin Phillips through to Jermain Defoe, the fans have always craved a star. Thomas Sorensen, Julio Arca, and briefly Darren Bent, are amongst those who have been admired and adored, while the two Jordans: Henderson and Pickford, have been the best of the home grown talent.

One man stands head and shoulders above all others in the opening two decades at the Stadium of Light: Niall Quinn. His contribution commenced as a tremendous centre-forward who formed a magical partnership with Kevin Phillips as Sunderland excited and entertained in the first few years of the stadium. Maybe naively, some people hoped that life at the Stadium of Light would always be like those golden early days when Quinny's strike-partner SuperKev won the Golden Shoe as Europe's top scorer. When those glittering years came to an end with the club at a very low ebb, the easiest thing in the world for Niall to do was to get on with his life as a player who had hung up his boots. Not a bit of it, he pulled together a consortium of mainly Irish businessmen to take over the club and lead the Lads into another glorious era - this time Niall being the front-man off the pitch, briefly as manager, but more successfully as chairman, having installed the 'box-office' figure of Roy Keane as manager.

Having hosted top flight football in 15 of the first 20 seasons at the Stadium of Light, the Wearside public have seen the top stars of the era in action: Ronaldo, Beckham, Henry and Aguero are just some of the stars to have strutted their stuff at Sunderland. While the club rightly focusses on football, the Stadium of Light has also been host to the biggest stars in music: Take That, One Direction, Beyonce and Oasis being amongst the household names to have graced the Stadium of Light.

Undoubtedly the first two decades at the Stadium of Light have been dramatic and often delightful ones. In 2096, when the SoL is as old as Roker Park was when it closed, future generations will look back at the highs and lows of the opening 20 years of a stadium that has become an integral part of the life of everyone who calls themselves a Sunderland supporter. The place already has a history of its own. It is a history that will continue to grow and a history you are very much part of. Re-live the story so far in SoL 20.

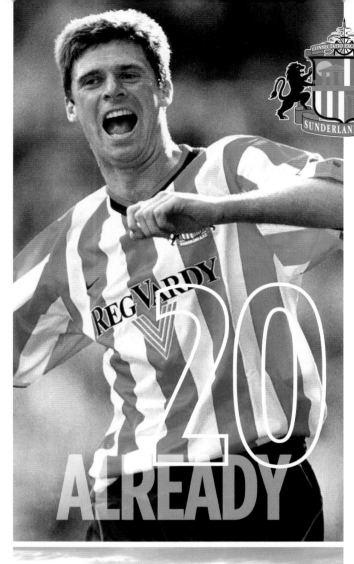

STADIUM OF LIGHT

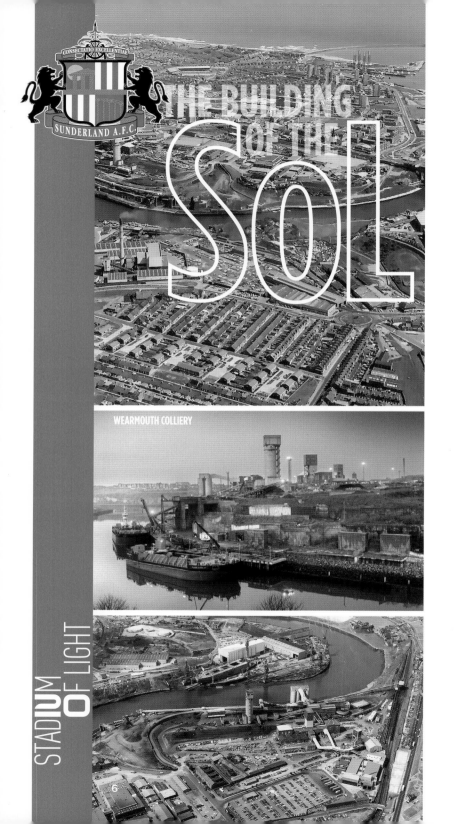

WEARMOUTH COLLIERY

THE BUILDING OF THE SoL

On 15 April 1989, 5,944 people saw Sunderland draw 2-2 at Oldham Athletic. 36 miles away at the home of Sheffield Wednesday, the Hillsborough disaster that same afternoon resulted in the unnecessary loss of 96 lives. The subsequent Taylor Report of January 1990 required all teams in the Premier League and Division One to have provided all seater accommodation by August 1994.

Sunderland played three full seasons after that date with standing accommodation on all four sides of an almost century old ground in Roker Park. The old Roker End; a shadow of its former self after being reduced to a third of its original capacity in 1983, was uncovered as it always had been, meaning that as the twenty-first century approached, the match-day experience of a Roker-Ender involved standing throughout and getting soaked if the weather was bad. Refreshment and toilet facilities were almost Dickensian, while the rest of Roker Park was hardly salubrious.

The Fulwell End was just like the Roker, except it had a cover put on it for the 1966 World Cup. The Clock Stand had ancient little folding wooden seats with standing room in front. The Main Stand had some grandeur, but it was dated. The club's offices and the limited space they had for entertaining was housed within this 1929 structure, but even in this poshest part of the ground, you might well take your seat to find there was a pillar obstructing your view.

Regardless of its limitations, Roker Park tugged on the emotional heart-strings. Having opened in 1898, supporters knew that their forefathers had stood at the ground. They had cheered on Charlie Hurley, Shack, Raich Carter and even before that, Charlie Buchan. There were a few old people about who had seen the league title won before the war and plenty for whom the days of the 1973 cup winners and Hurley's '64 promotion team were ingrained in their psyche.

In a lifetime most people move house several times, but your club's football ground stays constant throughout. The thought of leaving a place with so many memories shared by so many generations was not one many supporters wished to contemplate.

Bob Murray might have been sitting in the posh seats as Chairman, but he knew what supporting the club was all about. As a boy, Bob started in the Clock Stand as one of the little kids who stood on a bit of wood held on the front of the paddock railings with a couple of pieces of rope. The directors had the same emotional attachment to the old ground as anyone else, but it was they who were tasked with taking the club into the new century, just as almost a hundred years earlier Sunderland moved to Roker Park in 1898, having out-grown their previous Newcastle Road ground.

In November 1990, Chairman Murray announced that fans would be consulted on their views with regard to a new ground. Late the following year, it became known that the Football Association supported the club's intention to move and in 1992 a referendum was undertaken to measure opposition to a potential move away from Roker Park.

SAFC's vice-chairman Graeme Wood was tasked with examining several sites in the search for a new home for Sunderland AFC. The preferred site at Washington - within the boundaries of Sunderland - consisted of a 118.92 acre site, a gigantic expansion on Roker Park's eight acres. The stadium was to have a 48,000 capacity with 12,000 free car-parking places, plus a conference and exhibition centre. The proposed ground also had twin towers similar to the ones at the then still existing, but since demolished, original Wembley stadium. Rather like a striker who never signed, the Washington stadium was the 'one that got away' but while it had many pluses, arguably the failure of it getting off the drawing board was to the long-term benefit of the club. So often in the era clubs moved to the edge of town, away from their traditional base and this mostly proved very unpopular.

The result of the referendum indicating opposition from only 1,644 fans who had expressed a wish to stay at Roker Park, was announced the day before a home win over Wolves in November 1992, when only 13,500 more than the ballot number turned up.

Billed as 'the Wembley of the North' due to the grandiose twin towers, the proposed new stadium found opposition coming from Nissan who officially objected in March 1993. Nine months later, came the closure of Wearmouth pit where the Stadium of Light now stands.

Backed by the Tyne and Wear Development Corporation who were eager to reclaim the land, plans for Wearmouth to be the site of Sunderland's new ground gathered pace quicker than Duncan Watmore chasing a long ball.

SAFC commissioned a Feasibility Review of the finance raising opportunities for the construction of a new stadium. This report conducted by the Tyne & Wear Development Corporation reported in February 1995. At that time the team were struggling at the bottom end of what is now the Championship and manager Mick Buxton did not have long to go before he was sacked. It was a tough time to be thinking about money for a new stadium, let alone thinking big and planning a stadium to knock spots off the others being constructed at the time.

The Board knew that the clock was ticking. Under the terms of the Taylor Report the club had to demonstrate it was making significant progress towards re-developing Roker Park or moving to a new stadium.

THE SITE OF THE SOL IS CLEARED   ABOVE, THE PROPOSED NEW STADIUM AT WASHINGTON

DANGER DEEP EXCAVATION

ROKER PARK 1994

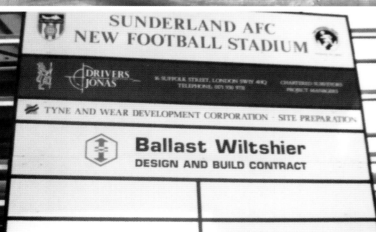

Without either, the club; who had been granted a year's extension in 1994, would struggle to qualify for a further extension to keep playing at Roker. In 1995, the capacity of the entire ground was a little less than the 23,000 that the Roker End alone once held. Without investment, the football authorities were thought likely to reduce the capacity to just 13,000 for the 1995-96 and 1996-97 seasons when 5,500 temporary seats were proposed to add to the existing seating of 7,500. Imagine a capacity of 13,000 as Sunderland were to win the league in '95-96 and play their first season in the Premier League in '96-97.

Having concluded that there was no point in investing significant sums into developing the existing ground, in the middle of a built-up area which seriously restricted the potential of such investment, it had been decided to look for a new site.

The site of what became the Stadium of Light was identified in the February 1995 feasibility study which confirmed that Bob Murray had agreed to underwrite all of the new equity requirement that was to be required for the financing of the project. Help from the Football Trust was also to be forthcoming with commercial sponsorship at that time anticipating potential stadium and individual stand naming rights.

To aid the new investment, John Fickling joined the Board on 18 February 1995 as a major share-holder, becoming vice-chairman. Aged 44 at the time, Hetton lad Fickling had first come to Roker Park as a six-year old.

The club stressed that the Wearmouth Colliery site had been found to be ideal and looked to quash uninformed rumours concerning its suitability, being the site of a former pit.

Chartered Surveyors Drivas Jonas and the stadium's architects The Miller Partnership (who had designed the new Ibrox, The New Den and Middlesbrough's Riverside Stadium) expressed their confidence and the stadium was announced as being developed structurally to reflect the three main features of the Sunderland area - Glass Manufacturing, Shipbuilding and Coal Mining with visual inspiration for the stadium being drawn from these sources.

Initially the plans for the Stadium of Light were for it to be an all-seated arena with a 30,000 capacity, albeit with the scope for subsequent enlargement. Original plans envisaged raising the capacity by 3,000 after two years. In the season the board were making these plans, Sunderland's average attendance was 15,389, but having been lifetime Sunderland supporters the board knew that in the past more than that number had been locked out of Roker Park when it held over 50,000 so they understood that if they built it - they would come.

An alternative plan put forward for a potential site at Ryhope near the hospitals was short-lived. Had that idea progressed the club could have crossed the river back to the south of

Sunderland where it began in 1879, but left for the north of the (then) town in 1883, never to return.

In August 1995, Environment Secretary John Gummer turned down calls for a Public Inquiry. This speeded up progress towards the new ground, but the Tyne and Wear Development Corporation still had to confirm it would support all that a new stadium entailed. Such concerns included managing traffic, parking and access. All major issues - as they had been with the Washington site - and especially near to the city centre.

Monday 13 November 1995 was described as 'a historic day' by Bob Murray as the TWDC granted planning permission for the stadium and within a month four construction companies were reported to have expressed an interest in building the stadium: Taylor Woodrow plc, Birse, Tilbury Douglas and the company who got the job as main contractor, Ballast Wiltshier who signed their contract on 25 April. They were part of the Ballast Nedam NV group who had built the Amsterdam Arena which opened the previous year and provided links with the Dutch club who became the visitors for the opening match.

The following March came important news of funding support as The Football Trust made a record contribution of £3.25m, mostly in the form of a grant. Meanwhile, Bob Murray had raised the bar and moved towards a capacity in excess of 40,000 which Environment Secretary Gummer agreed to in April. Murray signed an agreement to build the stadium at a cost of £15m.

More good news followed with the announcement that around 400 jobs would be created in building the stadium and within days, bulldozers and diggers arrived on site as the TWDC began routine clearing up of the former British Coal land. Reclamation work duly completed, 26 June 1996 became another important milestone as Bob Murray officially accepted ownership of the site. Amazingly, just 13 months and four days later, SAFC were playing their first game at their new home.

Working with English partnerships which led the government's regeneration strategy, the TWDC invested £1.7m in the Stadium Park Development while English Partnerships put in £8.9m for site preparation. This was a mammoth task as 50,000 tons of concrete foundations were removed and 350,000 tons of clay and soil were taken away as the bowl was created for the pitch to be laid below the surface of ground level. Old mine workings were removed, while along the riverbank the Grade II lime kilns were duly protected and would be reflected in the choice of the stadium name.

If you've ever bought a house, you'll know that arranging the finance is central to your plans and away from the hard-hats and bulldozers the costs had to be covered. Bob Murray's importance to the project was further highlighted by a £6m loan payable over ten years through a subsidiary of the Bank of Scotland. This was dependent upon Murray retaining a minimum 30% stake in the club for the next decade.

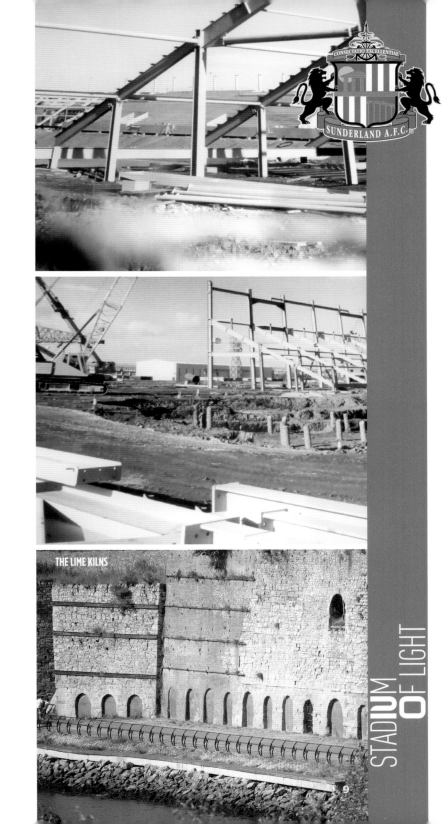

THE LIME KILNS

Infamously, Len Shackleton had dedicated a blank page in his autobiography to 'the average director's knowledge of football', but evidently Murray wasn't your average director and made the inspired decision to ask the 'Clown Prince of Soccer' himself to come and open a visitor centre for the stadium. Situated at what is now the South Stand, the centre allowed supporters to come and view plans of the stadium and watch it grow.

Many fans came to the centre on a weekly basis, just as they would regularly return to Roker as it faded into history, a planning application to the City Council to transform it into housing being submitted just as the SoL visitor centre opened. The following February, Wimpey Homes purchased the land where you can now buy a house and live on the site that Gabbiadini, Rowell, Sharkey and the rest once used to star.

Steelwork started to rise on the site of the new stadium as early as August 1996. By October, around a third of its outline could be seen and by the end of the year the roof started to become visible. In order to maximise stadium space, the club also built the administrative block which in time became known as Black Cat House.

The pitch was already growing as seats started to be fitted in February, by which time 22,000 had already been reserved. By March 1997, with the clock ticking towards the following season being at the new stadium, the internal fit-out of the venue was underway. Dressing rooms, media facilities, corporate areas and the club shop were all under construction.

Every minute was used as contractors and staff worked around the clock to get things done on time. As midnight ticked past on the day the stadium was due to stage its opening game, Bob Murray and John Fickling took to the stage in the Sports bar to announce it would be called the Stadium of Light. In fact the lights were still on as in the bowl of the stadium many a last-minute task was still being carried out. For instance, Perspex roofs were being put on the dug-outs and a huge clean-up operation was under way.

To the immense credit of everyone involved, that very evening Sunderland's new stadium was packed to the rafters as Sunderland played the first of what will be something in the region of 2,500 matches there, should they stay for a hundred years and average 25 home games a season. Two decades on from the first match, it's easy to turn up and take the Stadium of Light for granted, but thanks to the vision and commitment of the directors in the final chapter at Roker Park, Sunderland supporters have a first-class stadium to call home.

10

SO WHY IS IT CALLED THE STADIUM OF LIGHT?

The sale of naming rights had been an important part of the planned finance of the building of the stadium and at some point in the future it is entirely possible that, like the stadia of Arsenal or Manchester City for instance, the Sunderland Stadium of Light may be renamed due to commercial sponsorship. The Board however weren't prepared to give such a prestigious prize away for anything other than major investment.

As Bob Murray and John Fickling stood before the assembled press and guests, in the Sports Bar at midnight on the night before the first game to reveal the stadium name, everyone expected it to be sponsored. As the directors gave their pre-amble to the naming and references started to emerge concerning light and shining, it was thought that perhaps it was going to be named after the battery manufacturers Ever Ready. Given it still wasn't quite finished, wags were ready to nickname it the 'Never Ready' stadium, although in fact when the real name was announced, it didn't take long for its mickey taking moniker to arrive.

A common misapprehension, then and now, is that the Sunderland Stadium of Light is named after Benfica's Stadium of Light. This is not true. To start with, Benfica's ground is not named the Stadium of Light. Its real name is the Estadio do Sport Lisboa e Benfica. The Stadium of Light is its nickname, just as in Milan, the stadium shared by Inter and AC Milan is not called the San Siro. That is the nickname of a venue correctly called the Guiseppe Meazza Stadium. In Lisbon the area Benfica's ground is in is called 'Luz' meaning Light, hence its common, but not official name.

Sunderland's Stadium of Light has more significant meaning. The name ties together several connections. Built on the site of what was once the deepest pit in the world, the name pays homage to the miners who worked there. They depended on their miners' lamps to show the way forward and the safety lamp used by the miners was invented by Sir Humphrey Davy in the Durham Coalfield. Furthermore, the inventor of the incandescent electric lamp, Joseph Swan was born in Sunderland and indeed there is a Swan Street named after him close to the stadium.

Additionally, near the stadium stand lime kilns from the glass-making heritage of Sunderland, the city in which The National Glass Centre stands just a little further along the River Wear from the Stadium of Light. The link here is that footballers are always in the lime-light and light illuminates the way forward.

There is no religious significance to the club, other than the Bishop of Durham blessed the stadium on its opening night. However, in a city which has no cathedral, the Stadium of Light is a place that the most loyal of fans have shown deep faith in. For all these reasons, the name the Stadium of Light is a name, that while it took time to grow on many people, is now a source of pride, just like the stadium itself.

SOL 20 memories of the Chairman and Vice Chairman of the time,

Sir Bob Murray CBE and John Fickling

Sunderland began the new century with a new stadium fit for it, soon followed by training facilities to match. If for a moment you envisage Sunderland in 2017 still struggling on at Roker Park, the financial cost of building a stadium, now combined with how far the club would have fallen behind, does not really bear thinking about.

"We could have been history as a club" says John Fickling Vice-chairman and Chief Executive at the time and still a season card holder. Fickling knew what more and more fans have come to realise: "Bob Murray is very visionary and at that time, it was obvious that the club had to move."

Asked what it meant to him when the whistle blew for the opening game and he could see his vision brought to fruition, Murray's first thoughts are not ones of relief, but of the people the stadium was built for. With a deep passion for the North East he says, "Sunderland has a great history and some very special people have supported the club for over a century and I mean really good people. A lot of these people don't have a lot going for them in their life and that's not their fault. I wanted those people to have the very best and to have something to be proud of - a sporting cathedral. It was a big stadium and the most important thing is, we filled it. My dad was a coal miner at Silksworth and I loved these people. I never took a salary or a dividend out of the club, nor an expense. I just wanted the best for the very special people who are Sunderland's supporters. I know I wasn't popular from time to time, but that didn't matter to me, I love the club and that's what mattered".

Having been coming to Roker Park since the mid-fifties, the chairman of the day knew all about supporters' emotional attachment to Roker: "My dad took me to the match. We went into the Clock Stand where my dad had two ropes [hooked onto the railings] and a little step so I could see" remembers Murray.

However, he knew the club had to look forward, "We only had a capacity of 23,000. The facilities were 100 years old. Time had moved on. I left my father at Roker Park, so I have all those memories as well, but you have to think about where the club is today and where you want it to be tomorrow. It cost me a lot of money to build the Stadium of Light, through share dilution or by putting money in. What I wanted was the best for the city and for the North East."

"Bob had the vision and I was the practical guy" says Fickling. "We were two life-long fans and it was fate really that brought us together. It was also fate that at the time, the Tyne and Wear Development Corporation were clearing the site of Wearmouth Colliery as part of their brief. Being an engineer I knew that sentiment aside, Roker Park was finished.

"Putting seats in was not going to work. Even as a fan, I had a business head on and could see Steve Gibson at Middlesbrough had demonstrated that. He was a big help to us."

Having been like a black cat on a hot tin roof sorting a million problems as the SoL was constructed, as kick-off arrived in the opening game John Fickling reflects, "It was very emotional, to the extent that I nearly had a tear in my eye. Everything just came together. In many ways it went even better than we could have visualised."

Both Bob and John recall the months leading up to the opening with the clarity you get from people for whom such an event is a major part of their life's work. Both remember it as if it was yesterday and continue to speak about the creation of the stadium with the passion and pride they both have carried for the club all their lives.

"Because of the time-scales, we got dispensation from the Football Licensing Authority for a further twelve months at Roker so the deadline for the start of the 1996-97 season was very much a race against time and some of the finer details progressed as we were going along" remembers John Fickling. "The early part of the build process saw TWDC clearing the land which wasn't so much a brown-field as a black-field site. They kept clearing bits and finding bits of shaft.

"I used to come over and look through the fence like a lot of people did. I was conscious that we were ending up with this big bowl. It suddenly dawned on me that this was a natural amphitheatre and we had a lot of cost saving if we could utilise that, because in essence you were reducing a third of the amount of steel you needed. So part way through the process we took that on board. By having the bowl we suddenly had this great opportunity commercially whereby all the players' facilities could be put below ground. Normally a stadium loses prime corporate areas in the centre of the main stand for these facilities. We put the drug-testing room in and a female officials' dressing room, which at the time was ground breaking stuff."

Bob Murray explains, "We had got planning permission for around 35,000, then got that increased to 42,000, before we started to build, and then we extended it to over 48,000 virtually the minute we finished it. People asked, 'What do you want a stadium that big for?' but my responsibility as chairman was to lead and take these decisions. I was absolutely comfortable about having a capacity of over 48,000. It was a 'no-brainer'".

"Fairly early on in the design process we thought 'Let's not go for 30,000, we thought let's go for 42" concurs Fickling, who adds,"It didn't mean a massive design change. It just meant you went out another couple of metres and in terms of the relevant costings the difference was marginal so the stadium evolved over a period of time."

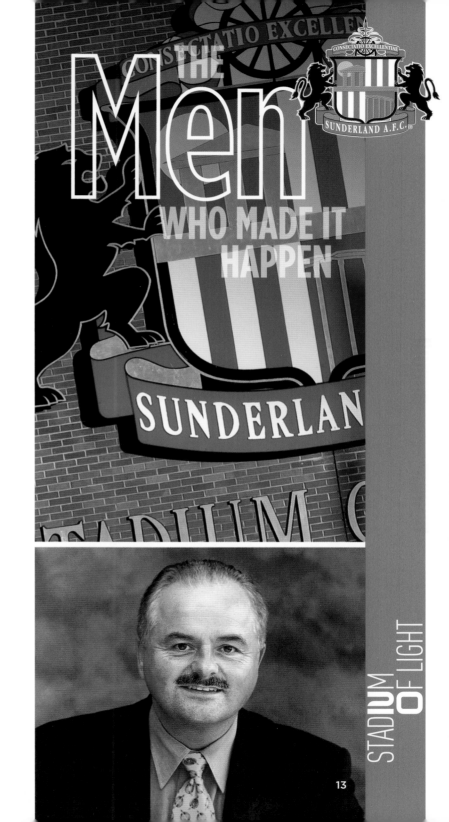

BOB AND JOHN AFTER THE RAIN-SOAKED DERBY VICTORY AT ST. JAMES' PARK IN 1999

Bob Murray hopes the stadium still isn't finished. "We had the planning permission to go to 55,000. I've left the land and the design at the club and I'm hopeful that one day it will go to 66,000. The same can be done to the rest of the stands as we did to the North Stand. You would then have a wrap-around stadium of a massive scale, but without 14 floors to climb up. I hope someone does that someday."

"We wanted to design the stadium in a way that it was easy to extend" agrees Fickling. "The concept was you could continue the top tier around and eventually end up with between 60 and 70,000. We wanted to be ambitious and not get the club into the position it had been in at Roker Park, where eventually the capacity was too small. We also wanted to keep the stands close to the pitch and fan-friendly with ample facilities for women and kids. 30% of the toilets on day one were female, but it was the right thing to do to create this family environment. Part of the design criteria is that we asked the architects to reflect the heritage of the city, so if you stand at the far side of the car park outside the main stand and look up, the top of the stand is done to try and replicate the bridge of a ship with the two balconies at either side. Some people might think that's a bit far-fetched, but that's how that came about."

Six years after the Stadium of Light opened, the Academy of Light followed. "I wanted to create the Stadium and the Academy of Light" says Sir Bob. "Both were equally important in my view. Every manager that comes remarks on the great training facilities. It was important that they were both built within a very short time so that the club had everything for the next 100 years. The priority for me was the Stadium of Light. I wanted to build it and leave a legacy in the city. I came into football to hopefully make a difference. The club were never ever in trouble. It was held in high esteem and I wanted the best ethics and the best standards in football to go with a first class stadium."

John Fickling recalls, "We were running in parallel with wanting to move to a new training ground as we were under a lot of pressure to improve the facilities at the Charlie Hurley Centre. We purchased the farm which is now the academy, subject to planning. At the time we had so much on we then parked that up in order to concentrate on the stadium. From day one, I was very involved in terms of the concept and design. The brief was that we wanted to satisfy all recommendations and FIFA requirements. The pitch is bigger than Roker Park. We wanted a stadium for the club and we had ambitions of getting into Europe and hosting internationals. We learned a lot from visiting other stadia."

Even now Fickling and Murray's knowledge of the SoL surpasses that of anyone else. The former enthuses, "There were FIFA guidelines about the minimum distance between the touch-line and the dug-outs and we satisfied that.

"That's why the West Stand is slightly further from the touch line than the other stands. The orientation of the pitch was done to make sure all of the mine shafts are outside the playing area. That's why the pitch is slightly north-west to south-east.

"An idea I came up with, was under-drawing the roof. This was due to the problems of pigeons. It had been an issue at Roker with just a few thousand seats so we decided to put sheeting under the roof. Not only did it solve the pigeon trouble, but it also made for better acoustics and externally it meant that the steelwork you saw was on the outside of the stadium which was a lot more impressive"

With no pun intended, given the stadium sits on the old Wearmouth Colliery, Fickling is a mine of information, "The pit originally drew water from a small well just the other side of the miners' lamp, so we tapped into that. We put a stop on it and put a duct in so that if there was ever a water shortage we could draw on the old pit well to draw water in for the pitch.

"I was dealing with the Safety Committee, the police and the council. We were meeting virtually every day as it got closer to the opening game. It was about 3pm on the day of the game when we got the stadium licence and it was nearer six when we actually got the liquor licence.

"On the afternoon of the Ajax match we had a leak in a pipe above the home dressing room. Yellow liquid was coming through and I thought, 'Bloody hell it looks like it's a pipe from one of the loos, but somebody must have plucked up the courage to test it and it turned out it was lager. I can remember Reidy was over the moon. He said, '**** great! Draught lager in the home dressing room!' That was Reidy all over."**

THE LADY DI STADIUM

Much was said about the name The Stadium of Light, but Sir Bob Murray explains it could have had another name, "We sought opinion from people. The vast majority were for Monkwearmouth or New Roker Park or Millennium Stadium.

The government rang up when Princess Di died and asked if we would re-name it 'The Princess Di Stadium'. I didn't feel that was appropriate and thought that the name we came up was more appropriate.

With our forefathers working in the dark along with the fact that Sunderland-born Joseph Swan had invented the incandescent light bulb, combined with the history of the Davy Lamp, we felt that we wanted to light the way forward. People talked about the name being the same as Benfica, but the Benfica ground is known as that because there is an area called Luz, which means light. Ours was an original name with good reasons behind it."

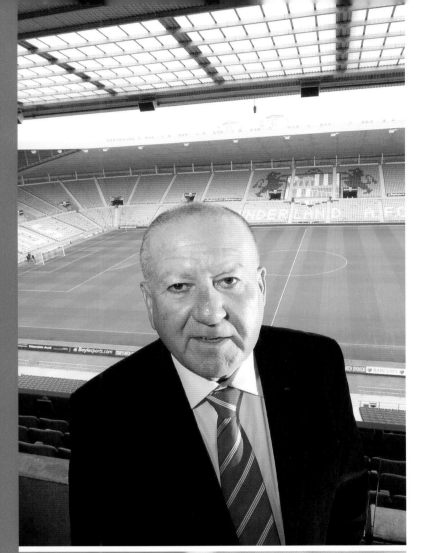

HRH PRINCE ANDREW OFFICIALLY OPENED THE STADIUM ON 10 NOVEMBER 1997.

15

NIALL QUINN CLEARS FROM ROB WITSCHGE

Opening NIGHT

TEAM LINE-UPS

SUNDERLAND

Perez (Zoetebier), Williams, Scott, Bracewell (Johnston), Ball (C) (Rae), Melville, Gray (Byrne), Ord, Quinn, Phillips (Bridges), Clark.
Unused subs: Smith, Howey.

AJAX

Van der Saar, Melchiot (Tobiasen), Blind (C), Oliseh, F. De Boer, R. De Boer (Reuser), Dani (Juan), Witschge (Sier), Babagida (Gorre), Sibon, Laudrup.

16

The Stadium's first game kicked-off moments after the unusually scheduled time of 8.10pm, some 20 hours after it was named, the Stadium of Light. Visitors Ajax were invited, due to the fact their year-old Amsterdam ArenA had been built by the parent company of Ballast Wiltshier, the company responsible for building the Sunderland Stadium of Light.

As Sunderland won the FA Cup in 1973, the Ajax of Johann Cruyff were winning the European Cup for the third year in succession. They had added a fourth title in 1995, winning the World Club Cup the year before opening the Stadium of Light.

Coached by Louis van Gaal, the Ajax line-up were full of big names including the de Boer brothers while Sunderland had a Dutchman of their own making his debut in goalkeeper Edwin Zoetebier. He came on at half time - when Sunderland re-emerged wearing their new mustard coloured away kit, allowing Ajax to be seen in their iconic white and red strip. The game finished goalless, although Kevin Ball thought he'd got the first goal only for it to be disallowed by Teesside official Jeff Winter.

A capacity 42,000 lapped up the action even though at kick-off there was much last-minute seat-rearranging when it emerged there was no row 36 due to a contractor mis-numbering the seats in the hurried frenzy of getting the stadium ready.

A two hour-long build-up gave the match a carnival atmosphere. Wembley Stadium MC Steve Kemsley had been drafted in to over-see proceedings which began with football juggler Rob Walters, plus the Ipi Tombi dancers and the kids of Sunderland.

The Shekinah Gospel Choir then followed a ceremonial Blessing of the stadium by the Bishop of Durham, before pop performances by bands called Orange, Orange, F.K.A. Upside Down, Clock, Kavana and Code Red.

Rock royalty Status Quo then arrived by military helicopter and performed on a red and white striped stage before the match ball followed them out of the skies, being delivered by the Red Devils parachute team.

The evening ended with a massive fireworks display. The real fireworks of course were to come when the real stuff started. The opening night however had set a standard of expectation for the fans, who after seeing the stadium rise now had experienced it for themselves. It was barely a quarter-of-a-mile away from Roker Park, but it was a world away in terms of all it had to offer. Roker Park had been a place those who had known it would always love, but Sunderland supporters had now seen the light.

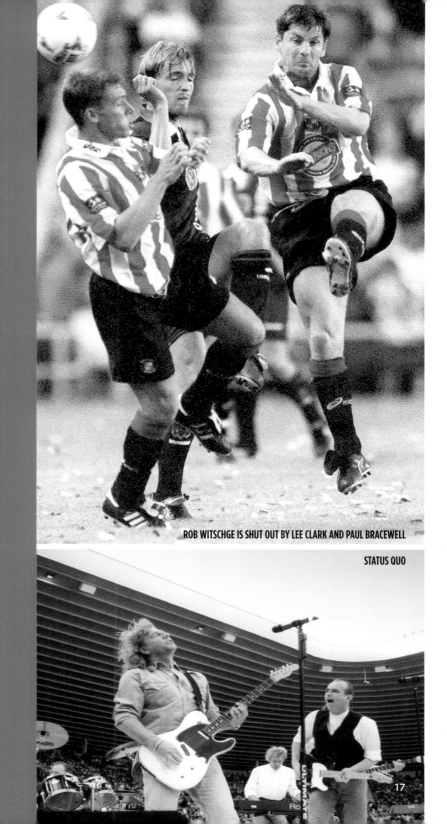

ROB WITSCHGE IS SHUT OUT BY LEE CLARK AND PAUL BRACEWELL

STATUS QUO

17

PLAYER OF THE YEAR
SuperKev Phillips

47+1 appearances · 35 goals

Is it any wonder the new signing most people hadn't heard of was Player of the Year as he broke Brian Clough's post-war scoring record? Breaking that record at Wembley, sadly SuperKev had to limp out of the Play-Off final otherwise the Lads may well have won.

Following the razzamatazz of the opening game v Ajax the real business got going once the league started. The first competitive match at the Stadium of Light was with Manchester City.

It was the most glamorous fixture newly relegated Sunderland could ask for. City had been the opponents in the game voted the best ever at Roker Park. A Sunderland Echo poll had concluded that City's 1973 cup game was the best seen in the 99 years at the former ground. City had finished in the bottom half of the Nationwide Division One (What is now the Championship) the year before, but were still as big a name as any in the division - apart from Sunderland themselves. Twenty years on, even ardent Sunderland fans might challenge that Sunderland are a bigger name, but this was before the mega-millions hit City, who then were still at Maine Road, not a spanking big new stadium like the Stadium of Light. And remember that even after all their investment, as things stand in 2017, Manchester City have still been champions of England fewer times than the Lads.

The visitors were managed by Frank Clark - Sunderland's assistant manager when promotion was won in 1980, while Sunderland manager Peter Reid was a previous City manager and player.

City's date with history at the Stadium of Light was 15 August 1997. It was a Friday night - Sunderland's first Friday night home game for 20 years. The division's highest attendance for almost a decade - 38,827 - meant that kick off had to be delayed from 7.45pm to a minute past eight, but once the game got going Sunderland wasted no time in tearing into the visitors.

Former Manchester City man Niall Quinn was never far away from a headline in his time at Sunderland and wrote his name into history books such as this one with the first goal at the ground. Always one step ahead, Quinny read Tony Vaughan's 16th minute back-pass, intercepted it and slotted it beyond 'keeper Martyn Margetson.

Before half time former 'Boro man Alan Kernaghan had obliged in helping Sunderland get the Sol off to a good start by getting himself sent off for two yellow cards. Of course, Sunderland being Sunderland nothing could be done simply and there had to be a bit of drama, so it came as no surprise when ten-man City levelled with under quarter of an hour to go.

The goal came when their star man Georgi Kinkladzi won and converted a penalty. It was a goal he deserved having been City's best player and hitting the bar earlier in the game. Beyond all the attention based on the new stadium Sunderland had promotion to win.

1997.98

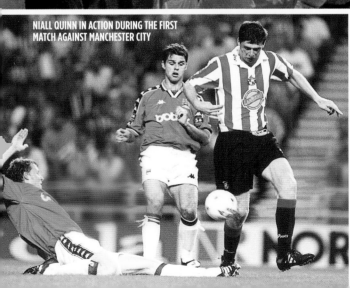

NIALL QUINN IN ACTION DURING THE FIRST MATCH AGAINST MANCHESTER CITY

MANCHESTER CITY'S GEORGI KINKLADZE WEAVES HIS WAY THROUGH THE SUNDERLAND DEFENCE

1997 98

MICHAEL GRAY CELEBRATES SCORING
THE WINNING GOAL AT BIRMINGHAM CITY

They had lasted just a solitary season in their first venture into the new Premier League and now that they had a stadium to compete with the best, they wanted to be back in the top flight asap. Already they had lost their opening match at Sheffield United and just one point would have placed a definite dampener on this historic first night at the club's new home.

Quinn had already left his mark on the match and about to step up to the plate was a man making his debut. Quinny nodded down a Mickey Gray cross for Kevin Ball to fire in a shot Margetson could only parry. In a flash there was a nippy little poacher in red and white saying, 'thank you very much' as he buried the loose ball. Kevin Phillips had his first Sunderland goal. By the time he left the club six years later he was Sunderland's record post-war scorer. Many of the goals to be scored by the Phillips/Quinn axis were supplied by a man who came on as a sub for City that night - Nicky Summerbee.

Making his home debut was a man who had cost almost double the £1.3m paid to City for Quinn a year earlier. Lee Clark's life-time allegiance was betrayed the day he signed for Sunderland. Selecting what to wear before putting pen to paper for the Wearsiders, Newcastle-man Clark looked in his wardrobe and pulled out a suit that was fine black and white stripes. In time Clark's passion for his home town team would win out and cause his demise, but as a testament to his professionalism and passion for the game, whenever Clark pulled on stripes of the red and white variety, he invariably gave it all he had. He had quite a bit. A very canny player. There were some good times to come and Clark made the team tick. With a minute to go of the Stadium of Light's first league game Clark unleashed a 20-yarder that found the bottom corner. That match had been won 3-1 - just like City's 1973 visit that had been voted 'Match of the Century.'

Although Norwich brought a reality check by becoming the first visiting side to win at the Stadium of Light in the very next home game, defeats at the Stadium of Light would be rare in the early years. There would only be one more home league defeat in the rest of the season and one the year after. In the first four years of the Stadium of Light if you came to all 138 home league games you would only see Sunderland beaten eight times, with just one loss between October 1997 and November 1999. When managers talk about turning the stadium into a fortress, it is records like that which Sunderland need to re-establish.

The turning point of the first season came after a 4-0 hammering by Reading that left Sunderland in the bottom half of the table after ten games. Eliminated from the League Cup at Boro before the next league fixture, the response was a 16-match unbeaten run that lifted the Lads to fourth.

GOAL OF THE SEASON
Niall Quinn

Sunderland 4-2 Port Vale
31 January 1998

A delicate chip that floated over the goalkeeper as if in slow motion. Brilliant!

PETER REID AND BOBBY SAXTON

NATIONWIDE DIVISION ONE 1997-98

			HOME					AWAY					
P	W	D	L	F	A	W	D	L	F	A	Pts	Pos	
46	14	7	2	49	22	12	5	6	37	28	90	3rd	

Play-Off finalists: Lost to Charlton 6-7 on penalties after 4-4 draw.

FA Cup: 4th Round, lost 2-1 at Tranmere Rovers.

League Cup: 3rd Round, lost 2-0 at Middlesbrough.

ATTENDANCES

Average (league): 34,523

Highest: 41,214 v Stoke City, 25 April 1998.

It was a run that brought the stadium's first 40,000 gate (against Bradford City on Boxing Day) and one of the best matches in the stadium's history. The atmosphere in a 4-2 win over Sheffield United was the best at the stadium so far on a day when SuperKev became the first player in 45 years to score in a sixth successive game.

Phillips scored again when the Blades returned for the final match of the first season in a Play-Off second leg. Second for much of the closing stages, defeat at Ipswich in the final week meant Sunderland ended up third. 90 points had been achieved, normally a tally that would achieve automatic promotion, but this time it was a point short.

In the first leg of the Play-Offs they lost at Sheffield United as they had in the opening game of the season, but as in the Blades' first visit to the Stadium of Light, their trip in the Play-Offs was a thriller, SuperKev snatching the final goal in a 3-2 aggregate win.

At Wembley, a Sunderland-born player would score a hat-trick - but unfortunately it was against Sunderland. Charlton's Clive Mendonca did the damage on a day when Sunderland scored ten times (against a team who hadn't conceded a goal for nine games) and still lost! A 4-4 draw was followed by a 7-6 loss on penalties, Mickey Gray being the unlucky man to see his penalty saved by Sasa Ilic.

So the initial season at the Stadium of Light finished at Wembley. It had been a hell of a first year in the new era of Sunderland AFC. Top scorers in the division, a total of 102 goals had been scored, a new hero in SuperKev had emerged and crowd numbers had surged as 'Reidy's Kings' brought the feel-good factor to the Stadium of Light.

Things would get better still the following year when the Lads would waltz to the league title with even more points than the number of goals netted in this first campaign.

Inevitably, there have been bad and sad seasons since at the Stadium of Light, but it was the excitement and entertainment produced in those first steps at the stadium that showed the fans that even when the bad times have to be endured, after the stadium had been built with bricks and mortar, the building kept going.

The building that took place under Peter Reid and his coach Bobby Saxton was the building of belief. Managers and players have come and gone since then but the fans remain and they learned that the Stadium of Light could be a place to be proud of.

MATCH OF THE SEASON

Sunderland 2-0 Sheffield United

13 May 1998 · Play-Off 2nd leg
(Won 3-2 on aggregate)

1997-98

KEVIN PHILLIPS CELEBRATES THE
SECOND GOAL IN THE PLAY-OFF SEMI-FINAL
SECOND LEG AGAINST SHEFFIELD UNITED

SUPERKEV SCORES THE SECOND GOAL IN THE PLAY-OFF FINAL

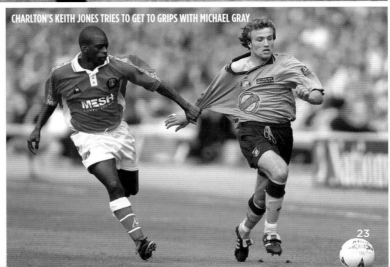

CHARLTON'S KEITH JONES TRIES TO GET TO GRIPS WITH MICHAEL GRAY

STADIUM **OF** LIGHT

23

98-99

ALLAN 'MAGIC' JOHNSTON

What a season this was. A record 105 points were achieved with only three of 46 league games lost. Runners-up Bradford were a massive 18 points behind, while there was an incredible 32-point gap to Wolves who were the first team outside the Play-Off positions. Twenty-five clean sheets were kept in the league with another five in the cups where Sunderland reached the League Cup semi-final.

With such a sensational season Sunderland didn't have to worry about the Play-Offs this time around. Following the gigantic disappointment of the previous campaign where after losing the Play-Off final on penalties and achieving 90 points, some players might have crumbled under their own self-pity. Instead, Sunderland stood up and just wiped the floor with a division they probably shouldn't have been in.

Straight after the Wembley defeat Peter Reid, Bobby Saxton and Niall Quinn had the Lads on the pop on the way home. Reidy had started his promotion campaign the second Sasa Ilic saved Mickey Gray's decisive shoot-out spot-kick. Consoling the crestfallen Gray, who needed lifting after a moment that could have ruined his career, but instead was the making of it (what doesn't kill you makes you stronger), Reid was magnanimous in defeat, congratulating victors Charlton and immediately set about instilling a belief in his players that promotion hadn't been missed, it had merely been delayed.

So often pictures of Peter, such as the ones of him leading Sunderland out at Wembley, have a reminiscence of Sunderland's first Wembley-winning manager, Johnny Cochrane in the 1930s. There's always also an element of the Jimmy Cagney about Reidy - the swagger, the confidence. Make no mistake about it, Peter Reid was a brilliant manager. Like all managers it ended in tears. Even Bob Stokoe's last days were dark ones, but when people criticise Reid for some of his later signings, such as Milton Nunez and Carsten Fredgaard, you also have to consider Thomas Sorensen, Kevin Phillips and Niall Quinn for a grand total of under £3m with all the add-ons included. You also have to remember these halcyon days that established the Stadium of Light. Look at the league record at the end of this chapter. For your season ticket money you saw Sunderland score 50 goals just in home league games and let less than one in for every two games.

It was swashbuckling stuff. It was a team made of partnerships. All over the pitch the team blended like the finest malts. On the flanks, Chris Makin and Nicky Summerbee on the right and Mickey Gray and Allan 'Magic' Johnston on the left were simply superb. Arguably, only David Beckham could cross a ball better than Summerbee at the time and Nicky needed only half a yard to whip one in. He wasn't a speed merchant or a trickster, he just delivered the ball quickly and for his target's first run.

A DELIGHTED MICHAEL BRIDGES AFTER SCORING AT BOLTON

GOAL OF THE SEASON
Michael Bridges
Sunderland 3-0 Luton Town
League Cup quarter-final · 1 December 1998
Brilliant curling shot at the North End.

QUINNY CELEBRATES SCORING
SUNDERLAND'S SECOND
AT HOME TO IPSWICH TOWN

PLAYER OF THE YEAR
Niall Quinn

42+4 appearances · 21 goals

In a team based on partnerships, Quinn was the focal point.
Get the ball to Niall and he'd score or set up SuperKev.
Injury-hit Phillips scored just two more than Niall who notched 21
in all competitions including one in the League Cup semi-final.

On the opposite flank, Johnston more than lived up to his nickname. In later years fans chanted, "You try to take the ball off Nyron, but he says 'no, no, no.'" In Johnston's case, if people tried to take the ball off him he might as well have said, "Now you see it, now you don't" as he conjured up a trick or two before either crossing, curling a trademark shot into the top corner or slipping the ball into the path of Gray who had zoomed passed him, getting around the back of the defence and causing havoc. Gray was like Patrick Van Aanholt getting forward, but unlike PVA, as keen to get back. With a team bursting with strong characters, there was no slacking from anyone. If there was they'd be out of the team as Reidy would bin them instantly, and in any case, Kevin Ball and co. would be having more than just words, on and off the pitch, with anyone not pulling their weight. Class and commitment. It's a simple recipe for success. Peter Reid had put it on the pitch and the league table shows that like many a good recipe, the proof was in the pudding!

Those partnerships weren't just on the flanks. The engine room was stoked by Bally and Lee Clark with Alex Rae dynamic in the two runs he got in the side. Newcomer Gavin McCann also got the odd game ahead of becoming a top midfielder. If anyone got past Bally there was the less than welcome sight of big Paul Butler and Andy Melville blocking the way at centre-back and then Thomas Sorensen in goal. Sorensen and Butler arrived at the start of the season and missed just three games between them.

Up front was the most famous partnership of all. Opposing defences had to mind their 'P's & Q's' when Phillips and Quinn were about. With a supply line coming in from both flanks and a probing central midfield the front two were the best seen in several generations. The 1973 cup-winners had flying wingers in Billy Hughes and Dennis Tueart with a battering ram of a great centre-forward in Vic Halom, but no Sunderland side in the era of twin strikers had been as good as Niall and SuperKev. They were what Len Shackleton and Trevor Ford could have been like in the fifties, if those two superstars from the days before superstars, had gelled together instead of infamously failing to combine.

And yet injury kept Phillips out of 20 of the 46 league games. He still managed 23 league goals from his 26 games though with Quinny getting 18 - one for every two of his 36 starts. Sunderland had proper strength in depth with yet another partnership at the ready in Michael Bridges and Danny Dichio. The brilliant young Bridges would end up going for a whopping £5m fee in July 1999 to Leeds United where he scored 19 Premier League goals in helping them qualify for the Champions League before sadly being badly injured.

It was typical of Sunderland. You wait an age for a top class goal-scorer and then two come at once.

1998-99

KEVIN BALL IN ACTION AGAINST WOLVES AT THE STADIUM OF LIGHT

THOMAS SORENSEN

MATCH OF THE SEASON

Sunderland 7-0 Oxford United

19 September 1998 · Nationwide Division One

LEE CLARK

STADIUM OF LIGHT

1998 99

STADIUM OF LIGHT

Bridges' path was blocked by Phillips, but when SuperKev was laid up, Bridges was 'Cool as Fridges' as the song went and kept the goals coming. There could only ever be one Niall Quinn, but when the veteran big man wasn't available 'Mellow-D' Danny Dichio called the tune. 'Deech' and Bridges were probably the second best front two in the division. Indeed when the Stadium of Light's record score of 7-0 was registered against Oxford neither Quinn or Phillips was in the side (Niall came off the bench) and both Bridges and Dichio grabbed a brace - Alex Rae getting two as well with Mickey Gray also getting in on the act.

A racing certainty all season, Sunderland sealed promotion with four games to spare, SuperKev scoring four in a 5-2 win at Bury where three sides of Gigg Lane were red and white. Afterwards in the dressing room big Niall gleefully smashed up the Nationwide League signs just as Sunderland had smashed up the Nationwide League.

Sunderland were long since ready to go up and on the day the trophy was raised, Republica came to the stadium to perform the 'Ready to Go' hit which had assumed anthemic status as the final part of the dramatic run-out music started by Prokofiev's 'Dance of the Knights.'

Kevin Ball wasn't going to miss out and talked himself out of a suspension to be able to play. Trailing 0-1 at home to Birmingham, Bally was having none of it and rattled anyone who needed rattling at half time. The other SuperKev wasn't going to lift a trophy after a damp squib of a defeat and he didn't. Phillips and Quinn turned the score around to 2-1 and as Bally one-handedly raised the trophy, everything that could have been done to cheer up Peter Reid had been achieved. In the lap of honour that followed, as Mickey Gray carried the trophy when he approached the main West Stand, the sound system turned to Chumbawumba's, 'I get knocked down, but I get up again'. It encapsulated what Sunderland is all about. The Stadium of Light is on the site of what was the biggest pit in the Durham coalfield. The supporters had seen a side fit to wear the stripes in honour of the history they were playing on, every time they stepped onto the pitch, and the biggest partnership of all in this glorious season was the connection between the players and the supporters.

That's what makes Sunderland so special. That's what Bob Stokoe meant when he said, 'Until you've seen football on the North East coast, you've never seen it.' That's why Sunderland got under Niall Quinn's skin and that's why you, as a Sunderland supporter, know that as the Stadium of Light reaches its 20th birthday, this is the Sunderland that one day must return.

PHILLIPS AND QUINN CELEBRATE

PETER REID

NATIONWIDE DIVISION ONE 1998-99

		HOME					AWAY						
P	W	D	L	F	A	W	D	L	F	A	Pts	Pos
46	19	3	1	50	10	12	9	2	41	28	105	1st

FA Cup: 4th round, lost 0-1 away to Blackburn Rovers.
League Cup: Semi-final, lost 2-3 on aggregate to Martin O'Neill's Leicester City.

ATTENDANCES

Average (league): 38,734
Highest: 41,634 v Birmingham City, 9 May 1999.

GAVIN McCANN FIRES IN A SHOT

NICKY SUMMERBEE

Looking back at the early years of the Stadium of Light, it's easy to recall that in the stadium's first two top-flight campaigns, the Lads earned back-to-back seventh placed finishes. What might be forgotten is that at the time those seventh places were disappointments. Oh how the Red and White army could do with being disappointed with such a position now!

In the first of the Premier League Stadium of Light seasons, Sunderland were third at Christmas - and a season later were second in mid-January. The first-ever Premier League game at the Stadium of Light was on 10 August 1999. Playing against his old club Watford, Kevin Phillips scored both goals in a 2-0 win, a penalty and a 'SuperKev Special' curler. It was a relief after the opening game had seen the 105-point team given a reality check as they were hammered out of sight at Chelsea. With future Sunderland head coach Gus Poyet to the fore, the Blues were unlucky to only win 4-0, but the Lads were quick learners and after that 2-0 response against Watford they kept another home clean-sheet as they held Arsenal to a goalless draw.

Narrow defeat at Leeds meant it was an okay start with four points from four games leading up to a derby at St. James'. Over the decades Sunderland had always been the more successful club of the North-East's big two. If anyone ever disputes that with you, ask them when the Magpies had ever held as many top-flight titles as Sunderland? They never have and if they ever win it again, they still won't have as many as the red and whites. Nonetheless, throughout the 1990s the Tynesiders had been in the ascendancy. The Keegan era had seen them playing in the Champions League and producing stylish attacking football while Sunderland struggled, sometimes struggling desperately.

Without a derby victory since 1990, Sunderland travelled to St. James' no longer the poor relations. Bob Murray's vision in building the Stadium of Light had lifted the stock of the Wearsiders while Peter Reid's acumen in building a team meant that Sunderland went to Newcastle with a better chance than they had for many a year. Nonetheless, undoubtedly Ruud Gullit's black and whites were strong favourites, but on a night where the rain was of biblical proportions, the tide turned as once again the Black Cats became the North-East's top dogs.

Newcastle's half-time lead was turned around when Quinn headed home a Summerbee cross, before the winger claimed a second assist when he sent SuperKev clear to show his class with a swivel and chip for a spectacular winner. Newcastle grumbled about the conditions and they grumbled about the team they had chosen - having left their star men on the bench

NIALL QUINN CELEBRATES AFTER SCORING
THE OPENER IN THE RAIN AT ST. JAMES'

1999·00

STADIUM **OF** LIGHT

1999-00

GOAL OF THE SEASON

Kevin Phillips

Sunderland 4-1 Chelsea
Premier League · 4 December 1999

Not just the goal of the season, one of the goals of the decade. SuperKev's 30-yarder at the South End was used on the opening credits for the following season's ITV highlights programme that replaced Match of the Day.

MATCH OF THE SEASON

Sunderland 4-1 Chelsea
Premier League · 4 December 1999

STADIUM OF LIGHT

PAUL THIRLWELL

32

JODY CRADDOCK

but Sunderland had a famous victory worth much more than three points. A long awaited derby victory and a Premier League away win instilled real belief into a team who had been used to winning week-in week-out for the previous two years at a lower level. This was lift-off and a trip into Quinn's bar at the Stadium of Light will show Peter Reid's rain-ruined jacket from that legendary night still on display.

The next away game was a 5-0 Premier League win at Derby - Phillips getting a hat-trick. It was followed by another 5-0 win at Walsall in the League Cup and a 4-0 Premier League victory at Bradford. 14-0 over three successive away games!

At home, a draw and four wins followed the derby, but the best was still to come. As Santa started to think of getting his suit dry cleaned for the big day, Sunderland found their Christmas had come early when Chelsea came north. Visiting fans' chants of '4-0' recalling the opening day of the season soon dried up as Sunderland roared into a 4-0 lead well before half time. Even without their first choice central midfield this was the day when everything went right. One up in 44 seconds, the goals just kept coming as Quinn and Phillips plundered a couple each. There had been big wins before, but with due respect to the vanquished opposition this was Chelsea Sunderland were taking apart – the same Chelsea who had welcomed Sunderland back to the Premier League with a lesson. That man Poyet pulled one back for the Londoners, but the message was clear that for the first time since the fifties, Sunderland had a team who deserved to be in the top half of the top flight.

One week later debutant left-winger Kevin Kilbane set up a goal in a routine 2-0 win over Southampton. Kilbane had a great career, but not at Sunderland where despite his great start he never consistently showed his best form. One of the nicest lads to pull on a Sunderland shirt in the Stadium of Light era, unfortunately for 'Chilla' he had the unenviable task of taking over from 'Magic' Johnston.

The previous season had ended with Johnston scoring in a special match to mark the 100th season of the Football League. As reigning Football League champions, Sunderland were invited to stage the showpiece against Liverpool, the league's record winners. While the visitors edged that match 2-3, Johnston's goal illustrated how much he had to offer in the big league. Sadly that never happened as a contract dispute left Peter Reid refusing to select either Johnston or Mickey Bridges.

Sunderland were also making a name for themselves in the top flight minus Lee Clark who had been at the heart of so much of their good play in the promotion season. Having worn his finely striped black and white suit on the day he signed for his boyhood club's fierce rivals, Clark had gone to see Newcastle in the FA Cup final.

CHRIS MAKIN

33

MANCHESTER UNITED'S ROY KEANE AND ALEX RAE

Nothing wrong with that, it's good to see a player passionate about his team. Lee was a good lad, but didn't have his brightest moment when on the day of the final he briefly agreed to wear a tee-shirt that was abusive to SAFC. Snapped in it, the picture was everywhere. It meant the end of his time as a Sunderland player. Lee later admitted he'd have found it difficult playing against Newcastle for Sunderland and again that was just him being honest, but what a shame it was that the contribution he made to the club should end so unnecessarily.

No matter how good they are, players come and go and regardless of the loss of key members of the promotion team, Reidy's red and whites were doing very well. Third after that win over Southampton a week before Christmas, it was as well that Christmas had come early as there was a horror show on Boxing Day. Future Sunderland man Don Hutchison dominated as Everton thrashed the Lads 5-0 for the first match in a run of eleven games without a win that dropped Sunderland to eighth, before Everton themselves were beaten on Wearside.

The start of that run had seen one of the stadium's best games and one of the greatest performances by a visiting player at the SoL. Two days after the Everton embarrassment a 2-2 draw with Manchester United witnessed future Sunderland manager Roy Keane show exactly why he was world class with an outstanding display.

Outstanding for Sunderland all season was Kevin Phillips who just kept finding the back of the net. In this one season SuperKev scored as many Premier League goals as Jermain Defoe did in his last two seasons at the club. Phillips' clinical finishing, his never-ending appetite for chances and his constant movement saw him score 30 goals, the last of them ending the Stadium of Light's first Premiership season on a high with a 1-0 win over West Ham.

PREMIER LEAGUE 1999-2000

	HOME					AWAY						
P	W	D	L	F	A	W	D	L	F	A	Pts	Pos
38	10	6	3	28	17	6	4	9	29	39	58	7

FA Cup: 4th round, lost at Tranmere Rovers (on a day when Rovers brought on a sub when they had a player sent off).
League Cup: 3rd round, lost 2-3 a.e.t. at Wimbledon.

ATTENDANCES
Average (League): 41,375 (Capacity 42,200)
Highest: 42,192 v Newcastle United, 5 February 2000.

SUPERKEV CELEBRATES GOAL NUMBER 30 AT HOME TO THE HAMMERS

PLAYER OF THE YEAR
Kevin Phillips

38 appearances · 30 goals

30 Premier League goals in 36 games made SuperKev the first Englishman to win the Adidas Golden Shoe as Europe's top scorer.

PHILLIPS GRABS THE EQUALISER AGAINST NEWCASTLE AT THE STADIUM OF LIGHT

STADIUM OF LIGHT

2000 01

MATCH OF THE SEASON

Sunderland 1-0 Arsenal

Premier League · 19 August 2000

...and away from the Stadium of Light, the 2-1 win at Newcastle in November.

ARSENAL'S KANU
IS CHALLENGED BY
DARREN HOLLOWAY

Many a promoted team do well initially, only to get found out and suffer the renowned 'second season syndrome.' Sunderland's second season syndrome meant they finished with fewer points than the previous year - but only one fewer as their seventh placed finish was repeated. If anything, this was a better achievement than the earlier campaign as they adapted to teams 'working them out'.

One man who did find it tougher was Kevin Phillips who scored under half the number of Premier League goals he contributed the previous season. Not surprisingly, opponents targeted the man who had been the continent's top scorer the previous year. SuperKev was still lethal, but the supply line to him was reduced. Phillips still scored a creditable 14 Premier League goals plus four more in the cups, but his goals needed to be replaced.

Niall Quinn wasn't getting any younger and again the supply line to the Irish legend was cut off as far as possible, Quinny scoring half the number of goals he'd managed in the previous campaign.

A goal-scoring midfielder can make a big difference to a team. In the first of the two seventh place seasons, Gavin McCann had been third in the scoring stakes with just four goals before a mid-season injury. This time around newcomer Don Hutchison doubled that tally, adding a couple more in the cup. His eight league goals being one more than Quinn.

In total the team were eleven goals shy of the previous season's tally. Peter Reid coped with this admirably. The man who had won the league on a shoe-string in his first full season in 1995-96 with a top scorer who scored 13 league goals but the tightest of defences, made Sunderland much harder to score against. While eleven fewer goals were scored, 15 fewer were conceded meaning that despite the front two contributing 23 fewer league goals the goal difference actually improved!

Further to the credit of the coaching staff this defensive improvement was despite the fact that former Arsenal defender Steve Bould had to hang up his boots after just a single appearance. As an experienced old-head Bould had been vital in the first half of the previous season.

Knowing the ex-England centre-back was coming to the end of the days Reid had unearthed a player who but for injury might have joined the list of stellar signings the manager made.

GOAL OF THE SEASON
Patrice Carteron

Sunderland 1-1 Newcastle United
Premier League · 21 April 2001

Long bursting run and superb finish at the North End in the biggest of games by the on-loan French full-back.

PLAYER OF THE YEAR
Don Hutchison

35+2 appearances · 10 goals

In his only full season at the club, the midfielder reached double figures in the scoring stakes - including one in the win at Newcastle.

Few, if any, supporters had heard of Slovakia international centre-half Stanislav Varga before he came to the club for a bargain fee, but 'Stan' was sensational on his debut as Arsenal were beaten 1-0 at the Stadium of Light.

The giant Slovak read everything, won the ball time after time and spread the play with a series of raking passes. Sunderland's clean sheet came with the help of another debutant as Austrian goalkeeper Jurgen Macho had to come on as a sub when Thomas Sorensen was injured.

Having found the stadium's 42,000 capacity was insufficient for the first successful Sunderland side in many a year, it had been a busy summer as the North Stand was extended. With a new top tier at that end taking the capacity to approaching 49,000. Varga and Macho weren't the only debutants as the North Stand upper was in action for the first time. With all this going on Niall Quinn wasn't going to be upstaged and popped up with the only goal of the game against his former club as Sunderland won on the opening day of a Premier League season for the first time.

Four days later calamity struck at Maine Road, then the home of newly promoted Manchester City where Paolo Wanchope got a hat-trick as Sunderland lost 4-2. What proved to be the final game of Bould's career was also the night that Varga picked up a serious injury and had to be replaced. He tried to come back a couple of months later, but wasn't right and ended up making only half-a-dozen more league starts that season, without ever looking like the awesome presence he had been in the best debut by a Sunderland defender in living memory.

For a while it looked as if Sunderland might have caught that second season syndrome as only one further point from the first five games had the Lads just one place outside the early season relegation zone.

Cash was splashed with Bob Murray backing Reid as he paid a club record fee for Brazilian defender Emerson Thome, signed young Argentinian Julio Arca and local lad Hutchison. The trio were seen at the Stadium of Light for the first time when that one other early point was picked up as Arca scored in a draw with West Ham United.

Coming with the nickname 'the Wall,' Thome strengthened the defence who soon produced a run of four consecutive clean sheets to stretch an unbeaten run to half-a-dozen games that lifted the Lads into the top half where supporters had got used to being!

2000 00 01

EMERSON THOME IS CONGRATULATED BY JULIO
AFTER SCORING THE WINNER AT HOME TO COVENTRY CITY

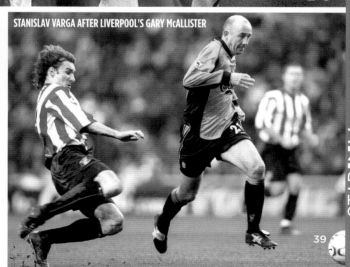

STANISLAV VARGA AFTER LIVERPOOL'S GARY McALLISTER

STADIUM **OF** LIGHT

THOMAS SORENSEN HEROICALLY SAVES ALAN SHEARER'S PENALTY

HUTCHISON LEVELS THE SCORE

40

It was mid-November though when the season caught fire. For the first time since the early thirties Sunderland secured successive wins at Newcastle. The home side took an early lead thanks to the much lamented Gary Speed and had chances to go further ahead as Sunderland battled to restrict them. As in the previous season a half-time home lead was overturned. Hutchison converted a SuperKev cross before a towering Niall Quinn header made the most of a Mickey Gray centre from a move that started with 'keeper Sorensen.

Despite the winner being a truly great goal, it isn't the main memory of the match. That accolade went to Sorensen for his tremendous late penalty save from Alan Shearer which protected a famous victory.

As in the season before, derby day delight sparked a terrific string of results. The next three matches were won in a run that ended up procuring 25 points out of 30. In the last victory of that sequence Sunderland were technically, briefly top of the Premier League for a few minutes in mid-January, on the day they won at West Ham, before results elsewhere meant they had to settle for second place.

Unfortunately, a bad run followed the good one. Just one win (4-2 at Chelsea) came in the next dozen matches before two late wins gave the Lads the possibility of qualifying for Europe on the last day. Despite a brace from Phillips in a draw at Everton that Holy Grail wasn't quite found, but of the 76 Premier League games played since promotion, 31 had been won and 23 lost. It was a good time to be a Sunderland supporter.

PREMIER LEAGUE 2000-01

	HOME						AWAY						
P	W	D	L	F	A	W	D	L	F	A	Pts	Pos
38	9	7	3	24	16	6	5	8	22	25	57	7th

FA Cup: 5th round, lost 0-2 at home to West Ham United.

League Cup: 5th round, lost 1-2 at Crystal Palace.

ATTENDANCES

Average (League): 46,832

Highest: 48,285 v Leeds United, 31 March 2001.

SORENSEN AND THOME CELEBRATE AT THE FINAL WHISTLE

PLAYER OF THE YEAR
Jody Craddock

30+1 appearances · 1 goal

Signed on the day the Stadium of Light opened, Jody Craddock gave the club excellent service and never more so than in 2001-02 when he played 30 league games despite missing a couple of months through injury.

SUPERKEV NETS HIS 100TH SAFC GOAL

In four seasons at the Stadium of Light there had been only good times. Disappointments yes, such as missing out on promotion in the initial season - although that disappointment came away from the SoL - but generally a day out at the SoL meant that more often than not you would go home happy.

Sunderland were used to winning. They were used to scoring. They were used to good football, and they were used to the craic from the manager, coaching staff and players being as good as the craic with their mates. Not in 2001-02.

The season started well enough. The first two home games were won 1-0 and on the day Kevin Phillips scored his 100th goal for the club, in a 2-0 win at Bolton as September ended, Sunderland sat in fifth place.

While SuperKev reached a milestone which only Len Shackleton and Gary Rowell had managed since World War Two, he was finding it harder to score. The front two of Phillips and Quinn were still there, but the old supply lines had long gone. Like so many of Sunderland's heroes of the past, getting a replacement for Niall Quinn was no easy task and Niall wasn't getting any younger as he continued to manage his potential back problem, often playing when he was nowhere near fully fit, but putting the team first.

French forward Lilian Laslandes had been brought in to be Phillips' new partner and debuted on the opening day. He had a record of scoring spectacular goals with his old club Bordeaux. The day after the awful terrorist attack on the World Trade Towers in New York, Laslandes got off the mark with a text-book header in a League Cup defeat at Sheffield Wednesday, but flopped in the league and was soon out of the side for good.

Niall soldiered on and incredibly managed to play some part in all 38 league games. He scored six valuable goals with Phillips top-scoring with 13, including one in each of the cups.

Goals were in such short supply that after the September game where SuperKev completed his 'Hot 100' there were only four more occasions where Sunderland managed more than a solitary goal in a league game. One of those occasions saw two set-pieces from Claudio Reyna, a USA international schemer Sunderland equalled the club record of £4.5m to sign from Rangers, but in the final analysis, a meagre 29 goals were scored in 38 league games. Home fans saw 18 goals go in the 'right' net - under one a game. It was a far cry from the 'goal-den' days the Stadium of Light had previously been used to.

Cameroon international Patrick Mbomba was turned to, on loan from Serie A outfit Parma. He bagged a beauty on his debut at Spurs, but never scored again.

Despite the drawbacks of the season enough victories were cobbled together to keep heads above water.

JODY CRADDOCK
SCORES THE SECOND
AT BOLTON

2001 02

STADIUM OF LIGHT

GOAL OF THE SEASON
Stefan Schwarz

Sunderland 1-1 Arsenal
Premier League · 27 October 2001

The Sweden international scored against his old club with a superb looping volley at the North Stand.

STADIUM **OF** LIGHT

44

Indeed, ten games were won and 40 points achieved. However on the final day of the season Sunderland, with just one point from their last four games, could conceivably have gone down. Thankfully, they took a point from a home game with already relegated Derby (for whom future SAFC 'keeper Mart Poom had a blinder) and with third bottom Ipswich losing at Liverpool, the Lads finished just above the drop-zone.

The season ended with a Benefit Match for Niall Quinn, with Sunderland taking on the Republic of Ireland, just before the Irish jetted off for the World Cup finals in South Korea and Japan. Niall played part of the match for both his club and his country. His Sunderland teammates Kevin Kilbane and Jason McAteer - who had arrived during the season - would join him in his nation's World Cup squad.

Although 2001-02 was a poor season, the club's raised profile since the move to the Stadium of Light was illustrated by the club's presence at the World Cup. One-time loan goalkeeper Shay Given was the only former player involved in the tournament, but Sunderland had six of their 2001-02 squad at the finals. In addition to the Irish trio, Claudio Reyna (USA), Thomas Sorensen (Denmark) and Patrick Mboma (Cameroon) flew to the Far East.

Moreover, a further nine players involved in the tournament would later play for Sunderland: El-Hadji Diouf (Senegal), Djibril Cisse (France), Ian Harte, David Connolly, Kenny Cunningham and Gary Breen (All Republic of Ireland), Wayne Bridge and Wes Brown (England) and Steven Pienaar (South Africa). Additionally, Republic of Ireland manager Mick McCarthy would later manage Sunderland, as would Roy Keane who failed to turn up for Niall's Benefit Match and then caused a huge furore by pulling out of the tournament.

With so many of the Irish squad later to come to Sunderland, as well as the three main men in McCarthy and Keane as well as Quinny, that 'Night with Niall' was to have red and white ramifications at the Stadium of Light in the seasons to come.

PREMIER LEAGUE 2001-02

		HOME				AWAY							
P	W	D	L	F	A	W	D	L	F	A	Pts	Pos
38	7	7	5	18	16	3	3	13	11	35	40	17

FA Cup: 3rd round, lost 1-2 at home to West Bromwich Albion.

League Cup: 2nd round, lost 2-4 at Sheffield Wednesday.

ATTENDANCES

Average (League): 46,745

Highest: 48,355 v Liverpool, 13 April 2002 (Stadium football record).

CLAUDIO REYNA

MATCH OF THE SEASON
Sunderland 2-1 Leicester City
Premier League · 1 April 2002

STEPHEN WRIGHT

In any history of a football club there are good seasons and bad ones. Even the currently most successful clubs have had their bad times. 2002-03 was certainly one of the worst in the Sunderland story. It was a culture shock for those who had started coming to the match since the building of the Stadium of Light. 2001-02 had been disappointing, but 2002-03 was much worse.

In a season when West Ham went down with 42 points Sunderland were rock bottom. Finishing with a club record low of a measly 19 points was bad enough, but what was staggering was that 18 of them had been garnered by a week before Christmas. At that stage Sunderland remained outside the relegation zone at the half-way point of the campaign.

Astonishingly, the second 19 fixtures yielded just a solitary point and that from a home goalless draw. Just two goals were scored in the final ten games in a season of three managers.

The sacking of Peter Reid early on marked the end of an era. Reid had straddled the closing of Roker Park and the opening of the Stadium of Light, but missed out on enjoying the benefits of the swish new training base 'The Academy of Light'. This opened in 2003, again through the vision and determination of Bob Murray (later Sir Bob Murray CBE).

Reidy had been in charge of 353 games - winning 60 more than he lost. No-one since has managed even half as many, and most nowhere near that. The manager had spent the summer pursuing the purchase of Robbie Keane, only for that deal to fall through, leaving Sunderland in urgent need of a new striker as Niall Quinn couldn't go on forever - not as a player anyway. Defenders Stephen Wright and Phil Babb had been brought in, along with Thomas Myhre as competition for Sorensen in goal. Speedy winger Matt Piper had also been bought, but with time in the transfer window running out, Sunderland swooped for a striker who made Laslandes look like a good buy.

Tore Andre Flo cost an initial £6.75m from Rangers. Much was expected of the ex-Chelsea man, especially when he got a debut goal against Manchester United at the SoL. There would be only three more league goals from him though - the last before the turn of the year - as he evidently wasn't up for the fight. The running joke was that the club shop had run out of the letter 'p' as fans added it to his name on the back of their shirts, while members of the press nicknamed him Tore Andre Four, as four out of ten seemed to be his common mark in the newspaper ratings. Also brought in was Marcus Stewart who had scored 19 Premier League goals for Ipswich just two seasons earlier. He would come good in time, but rarely got a start until it was too late.

02·03

20

MICHAEL PROCTOR CELEBRATES THE WINNER
WITH TEAMMATE GEORGE McCARTNEY

MATCH OF THE SEASON
Sunderland 2-1 Liverpool
Premier League · 15 December 2002

PROCTOR SCORES

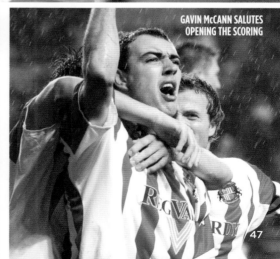

GAVIN McCANN SALUTES
OPENING THE SCORING

STADIUM OF LIGHT

47

20'02'03

STADIUM OF LIGHT

48

It was an edgy time at the club. Finishing 17th was not what the Stadium of Light had been built to see. Finishes of third and first in Division One followed by back-to-back seventh place Premier League positions were more like what the board of directors and the supporters had in mind when the new ground had been opened.

Seventh place had also been achieved a century earlier in the first season at Roker Park. but that had been followed by placings of third and second. In the fourth season at Roker the club had won the league. No-one had any serious thoughts that Sunderland were going to win the league now, but there had been a taste of being in the top two or three during the early days of the Stadium of Light. As unlikely as finishing top, in people's minds nor was finishing bottom, and Sunderland weren't just bottom, they were bottom by a country mile and increasingly the butt of jokes as the season wore on.

The beginning of the season wasn't actually that bad. A goalless draw at Blackburn on the opening day was a solid start. Certainly a 0-1 reverse to Everton in the first home fixture deflated fans, but within a week the gate had increased by 10,000 for the visit of Manchester United. Red Devils' fans like to chant' You've only come to see United' but in truth the home fans had been boosted by a mid-week win at old adversaries Leeds United and the prospect of seeing new signings Flo and Stewart, Flo getting a goal as a point was collected.

Three horrendous defeats followed and effectively made up the board's mind that it was time for a change. Beaten 3-0 at 'Boro and 2-0 at Newcastle, with the tamest of 3-0 home defeats to Fulham in between, Sunderland had slumped. Despite a home win over Aston Villa and the biggest away win since beating Newcastle 9-1 in 1908 (a 7-0 League Cup win at Cambridge) the end of Reidy's reign awaited. Defeat by 3-1 at defending champions Arsenal resulted in Peter Reid being told to clear his desk after acquiring only eight points from the opening nine games.

For the first managerial appointment in the Stadium of Light era Sunderland selected the last Englishman to guide a team to the top-flight title (a record he still holds as the Stadium of Light turns 20). The new boss was Howard Wilkinson, his assistant Steve Cotterill having given up the manager's chair at Stoke to come to Sunderland as number two.

Under 'Sergeant Wilko' there was a brief bounce. After a first game defeat at home to West Ham, an unbeaten five game run yielded six points, and an unlikely League Cup win at Arsenal.

Wilkinson's first match proved to be the last of Niall Quinn's career. Quinny had played on out of loyalty to Reidy, but like Len Shackleton, the first match of a new manager's reign also proved to be his final one as a player. The first home game after Niall hung his boots up saw the Irishman further illustrate his generosity.

PLAYER OF THE YEAR
Sean Thornton
14 appearances · 1 goal

The young Irish midfielder didn't make his debut until January, but offered a ray of hope in a season so dark that the Supporters' Association didn't name a Player of the Year. Thornton won the club's own award.

TORE ANDRE FLO CELEBRATES HIS EQUALISER

MARCUS STEWART

PREMIER LEAGUE 2002-03

		HOME					AWAY						
P	W	D	L	F	A	W	D	L	F	A	Pts	Pos
38	3	2	14	11	31	1	5	13	10	34	19	20th

FA Cup: 5th round, lost 0-1 at home to Watford.

League Cup: 4th round, lost 0-2 at Sheffield United.

ATTENDANCES

Average (league): 39,698

Highest: 47,586 v Manchester United, 31 August 2002.

Niall had raised £1m for hospitals in Sunderland and his birthplace of Dublin through his Benefit Match that summer. Quinn offered his thanks to supporters by donating a brand new car (a Vauxhall Corsa) as a prize to be given away to one lucky fan by means of a lucky number in the match programme at the next home game. That car could have come in useful a few years later when as chairman he organised the safe return of a plane-load of fans stranded at Bristol airport!

Quinn wasn't the only one leaving. Within the next few games Reyna and Schwarz made their final appearances as the quality count subsided in the Sunderland side. In a rare ray of light, Liverpool were beaten on Wearside for the first time since 1958, local lad Michael Proctor grabbing a late winner a few days before Kevin Phillips earned a point with a brace at West Brom.

As supporters opened their Christmas presents it was proving to be another season of struggle, but the Lads just had their heads above water, sitting one place above the bottom three. Anyone who received a 'part-season ticket' that Christmas morning may well be grateful for a pair of socks in future. Defeat after defeat after depressing defeat followed.

The worst run in the club's history (in fact it proved to be one game short of the worst run in any club's history in the final analysis) started with a bit of misfortune. Late goals contributed to some narrow defeats before that final point of the season arrived on 11 January.

Six defeats in seven games had all been by the odd goal until Sunderland somehow managed to score three own goals in losing 1-3 against Charlton Athletic in front of the long-suffering home fans. Three more losses and Wilkinson and Cotterill were gone, sacked while the reserves were mid-way through a game at Durham.

Into a hot-seat, now short-circuiting, stepped Mick McCarthy. A man who had had to deal with the circus surrounding Roy Keane's departure from the World Cup the previous summer, McCarthy was capable of dealing with a crisis and Sunderland certainly had one.

Try as he might, Mick just couldn't turn around the good ship Sunderland which was on a collision course with as many icebergs as it could hit. He oversaw nine successive defeats in a run of 15 losses in a row which ended the season. McCarthy's fourth game saw relegation mathematically confirmed at Birmingham, the ground where the last of the club's six league titles had been won at. Marcus Stewart was sent off that day for wiping out the show-boating future Sunderland forward Stern John. McCarthy made clear his approval of Stewart's actions.

The time for Sunderland to be a soft touch was over and there would be a lot more grit and graft in the team from now on. It was certainly needed after a season to write off - but sadly not even the worst one of the decade.

GOAL OF THE SEASON
Sean Thornton

Sunderland 1-2 Chelsea
Premier League · 5 April 2003

Thornton's volley highlighted an individual performance so good that Gianfranco Zola sought him out later to offer his shirt.

HOWARD WILKINSON AND STEVE COTTERILL

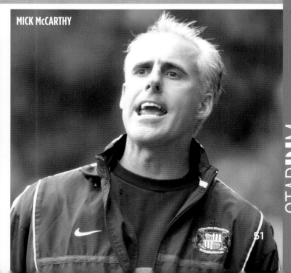

MICK McCARTHY

STADIUM **OF** LIGHT

JULIO ARCA CELEBRATES AFTER THE FA CUP FIFTH ROUND REPLAY EXTRA-TIME 2-0 VICTORY OVER BIRMINGHAM

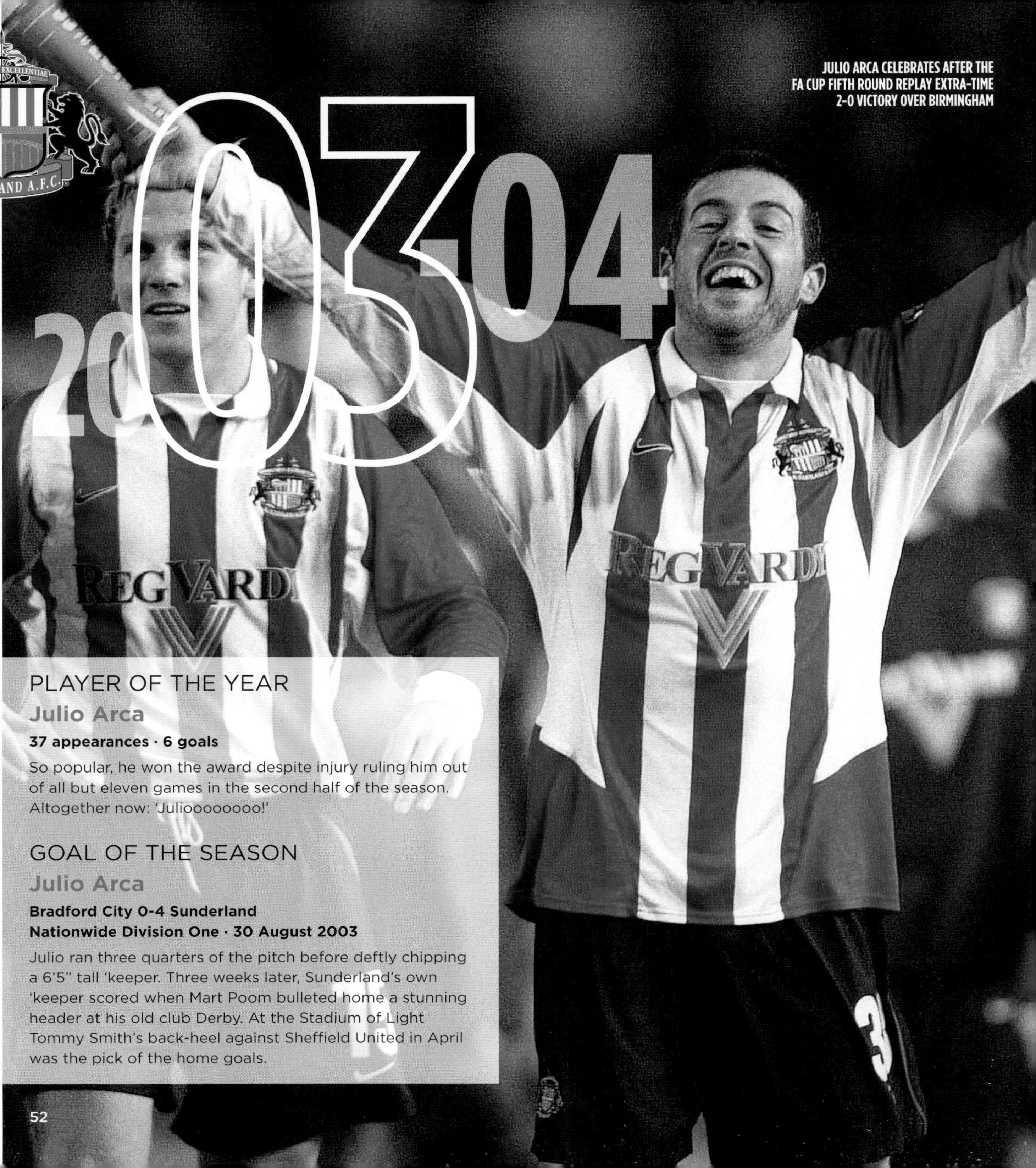

2003-04

PLAYER OF THE YEAR

Julio Arca

37 appearances · 6 goals

So popular, he won the award despite injury ruling him out of all but eleven games in the second half of the season. Altogether now: 'Juliooooooo!'

GOAL OF THE SEASON

Julio Arca

Bradford City 0-4 Sunderland
Nationwide Division One · 30 August 2003

Julio ran three quarters of the pitch before deftly chipping a 6'5" tall 'keeper. Three weeks later, Sunderland's own 'keeper scored when Mart Poom bulleted home a stunning header at his old club Derby. At the Stadium of Light Tommy Smith's back-heel against Sheffield United in April was the pick of the home goals.

No matter how bad things get in football, if you get yourselves organised and get stuck in, sooner or later things change. Mick McCarthy had taken on a big challenge to turn Sunderland around, but like Denis Smith 16 years earlier, he got hold of the club, gave it a shake and set it back down ready to start going in the right direction again. After the sinking spiral of the previous season, Sunderland needed Mick's no-nonsense approach.

Having overseen the sale of a huge number of players including Kevin Phillips, Thomas Sorensen and Gavin McCann, McCarthy brought in mainly freebies. but he knew the kind of characters he wanted. Gary Breen had given McCarthy good service with Ireland and agreed to come and captain the side. Breen was not everyone's cup of tea, but he was rock solid behind the scenes, a good captain and someone who, in a less high profile way than many, was to gain a real affinity with the club and its supporters.

Similarly, Jeff Whitley was never going to win any most talented player or specialist penalty-taker awards, but if being organised and getting stuck in was to be the order of the day, then Breen was going to be the organiser and Whitley was certainly going to be the one to get stuck in!

McCarthy had been happy to see the big names go, arguing that if they were as good as supporters stated Sunderland wouldn't have been bottom of the table. However, he had pinned his hopes on keeping Jody Craddock, so when news that the centre-back was to be sold on the day of a pre-season friendly at Hearts, the manager was crestfallen.

Losing the opening two league games without scoring took the run of consecutive defeats to a mind-boggling 17. Not surprisingly, the Stadium of Light was half empty for the first match of the season, under 25,000 seeing Millwall, one of McCarthy's old clubs, win 1-0. It wouldn't be the most disappointing defeat by Millwall that season.

In 1898-99, the first season of Roker Park, Lancashire side Darwen had lost 18 second division games in a row. The club had dropped out of the Football League at the end of their record losing sequence season. As Sunderland lined up at Preston for a live TV match, the TV company arranged for the modern day Darwen players to take their places, ready to see their club's century-plus record equalled by sorry Sunderland.

Enough was enough. First-half goals from Player of the Year Thornton and the man McCarthy had put his faith in - Marcus Stewart - gave Sunderland a long, long overdue win. The wait was over, the tide had turned. Just two days later, the Stadium of Light faithful witnessed their first home league win of the calendar year, Watford being beaten 2-0 as they had in the stadium's first Premier League game four seasons earlier.

GARY BREEN

53

CARL ROBINSON SCORES
THE WINNING GOAL AGAINST
CHAMPIONS NORWICH CITY

MATCH OF THE SEASON

Sunderland 1-0 Norwich City

Nationwide Division One · 4 May 2004

Already the Stadium of Light was creating its own history to be referred back to.

Suddenly the team that couldn't win, couldn't stop winning. A 4-0 victory at Bradford featured a goal of the decade contender from the ever-popular Julio Arca, before a fourth successive win propelled the Lads up to fourth. A last minute penalty winner from Marcus Stewart that day had radio commentator Simon Crabtree urging people to 'kiss your granny' but many would feel like kicking their granny instead when Palace turned up at the end of the season for a Play-Off semi-final, lost on penalties.

Eight of eleven league games were won as McCarthy laid the foundations of the new Sunderland he was building. By the turn of the year, the club were still in the promotion race, holding on to fourth position.

With neither Newcastle or Middlesbrough in the same division the season's only derby brought Hartlepool United to the Stadium of Light in the FA Cup. To their credit, Poolies brought the biggest away support ever seen at the Stadium of Light, 9,000 filling the South End and round into the East Stand.

Sunderland though, were to enjoy a good cup run - appropriate as a tribute to Bob Stokoe who passed away during the run to the semi-final where Millwall won 1-0 at Old Trafford. Sunderland would have qualified for Europe had they won that game as the Londoners went into the UEFA Cup, even though they lost the final to Manchester United who had also qualified for the Champions League.

Losing a semi-final is often said to be one of the hardest defeats to take, but there was another big disappointment to come. As in 1998 Sunderland qualified for the Play-Offs having finished third in the division, although on this occasion the Lads were well behind the automatically promoted Norwich and West Brom. The Canaries actually clinched the title at the Stadium of Light where they heard WBA had lost at Stoke to hand them the title, despite the fact they had just lost to a goal from the recently-arrived Carl Robinson.

Play-Off games have their own dramas. In the first season at the Stadium of Light the second-leg win over Sheffield United still rates as one of the stadium's finest nights, but in 2004, the Play-Offs were once again to strain the nerves, as they probably will again at some point in the future.

A bad-tempered Friday night first-leg at Selhurst Park saw Sunderland lose 3-2. As in the 2-1 win against Palace at the Stadium of Light early in the season, Sunderland's goals had come from a Stewart spot kick and a strike from Kevin Kyle. The big Scottish centre-forward had come through the ranks at SAFC. As a target man he was the replacement for Quinn.

The club had spent fortunes on in Laslandes and Flo and while Kyle was never going to be a 'SuperKev', he epitomised the quality of graft McCarthy had instilled into the team. 'Kyler' never hid his limitations.

KEVIN KYLE NETS THE SECOND IN THE PLAY-OFF SEMI-FINAL AT CRYSTAL PALACE CONGRATULATED BY JEFF WHITLEY, GEORGE McCARTNEY AND SEAN THORNTON

20 03 04

STADIUM OF LIGHT

20 03 04

MART POOM TURNS AWAY ARMS ALOFT AFTER HIS STOPPAGE TIME EQUALISER

He would never have the feather-like touch of Niall Quinn, but the lad gave it absolutely everything he had every time he pulled the stripes on - something he did 53 times that season. Both Kyle and Stewart would score in what remains the most recent Play-Off game at the Stadium of Light as it hits its 20th anniversary - the pair ending the season as joint top scorers with 16 apiece, Stewart having more in the league.

Joining them in the scorers list was goalkeeper Mart Poom. The regular number one had sensationally scored a last minute leveller at his old club Derby with one of the best headers in Sunderland's history, but as the Play-Off second-leg came to an end with the aggregate scores level, he faced a penalty shoot-out.

With the shoot-out score at 4-4, but with Sunderland having taken one more, the 'Poominator' saved from Shaun Derry when a goal would have defeated Sunderland. Into sudden death, 'Poomy' saved Sunderland again after Jason McAteer had his shot saved. The Estonian goalkeeper was finally beaten by Michael Hughes' decisive spot-kick after midfielder Whitley failed from the spot with Sunderland's seventh penalty - the same number that proved so costly to Mickey Gray at Wembley six years earlier. Whitley's 'twinkle-toes' run up passed into SoL legend. It was one of those moments that could make you cry and laugh at the same time - Sunderland supporters have had a few of those.

Ultimately the season ended once again in disappointment. Niall Quinn had yet to mention the Magic Carpet Ride, but the 2003-04 season had certainly been one. Sunderland had reached the semi-finals of both the FA Cup and the Play-Offs as well as finishing third in the table. Most importantly they had rediscovered a fighting spirit which had disappeared and there was a sense that the good times were near again.

NATIONWIDE DIVISION ONE 2003-04

		HOME						AWAY					
P	W	D	L	F	A	W	D	L	F	A	Pts	Pos
46	13	8	2	33	15	9	5	9	29	30	79	3rd

FA Cup: Semi-finalists, lost 0-1 to Millwall at Old Trafford.

League Cup: 2nd round, lost 2-4 at home to Huddersfield Town.

ATTENDANCES

Average (League): 27,119 (lowest in Stadium of Light history)

Highest: 40,816 v Hartlepool United, FA Cup 3rd round, 3 January 2004

Highest League: 36,278 v Walsall, 18 October 2003.

TOMMY SMITH AND JOHN OSTER

PLAYER OF THE YEAR
George McCartney
37+1 appearances · 0 goals

George edged the award from Julio Arca. The pair's left-flank partnership was the strongest part of the Championship winning team, with Northern Ireland international McCartney a real creator as an attacking left-back.

For the second time since moving to the Stadium of Light, Sunderland responded to losing on penalties in the Play-Offs by winning the league. The team of 2004-05 weren't in the same class as the 105-point side of six seasons earlier, but their achievement should not be overlooked.

Their 94 points was the same as Newcastle got after all the money spent by Rafa Benitez in 2017 and they were a more than comfortable seven points ahead of runners-up Wigan, and nine clear of Ipswich in the first of the Play-off positions. Thankfully, this time around, there was no need for the palaver of the Play-Offs for Sunderland.

McCarthy's men were a collection of modest buys. Amongst them were Dean Whitehead from Oxford United, Liam 'Lennie' Lawrence from Mansfield Town and Stephen 'Sleeves' Elliott from Manchester City reserves. All would debut in an opening day defeat at Coventry. Also coming into the side were ex-Newcastle centre-back Steve Caldwell and the two Collins'. No relation. Neill came from Dumbarton with Danny coming from Chester after he had played for them in an early season League Cup clash at the Stadium of Light.

Elliott partnered Marcus Stewart up front, the unlucky Kyle missing all but the opening month of the campaign though injury. Similarly, Caldwell linked up well with Gary Breen at the heart of the defence. In midfield, Carl Robinson wasn't as good as Lee Clark had been in the late nineties, but the Wales international was composed and possessed a touch of class. He also had a good football brain and linked the team by being a good communicator as well as a good passer of the ball, while Whitehead was the engine.

Chief creator was still Julio Arca who chipped in with nine league goals, two hat-tricks helping Stewart pip Elliott as top scorer; the pair getting 31 between them in the league. Player of the Year George McCartney was at left-back where he dove-tailed with wide man Arca, while ex-Liverpool man Stephen Wright was the regular right-back. In goal Thomas Myhre took over from Mart Poom in the autumn, but the injury-prone Norway international missed out on the run-in leaving Michael Ingham and subsequently youngster Ben Alnwick to get Sunderland over the line.

Crowd favourite Sean Thornton started only three matches as McCarthy constantly tried to moderate the midfielder's lifestyle to get the best from his talents. Thornton was a regular sub as was another crowd favourite - Mickey Bridges, who had returned for a second spell, his career having been blighted by injury. Based on talent and professionalism, Bridges by now should have been a household name and England international, but you need luck as well as ability and attitude to be a success in football.

GOAL OF THE SEASON

Sean Thornton

**Sunderland 4-1 Rotherham United
Nationwide Division One · 22 February 2005**

Having come off the bench to replace set-piece specialist Arca, Sean Thornton curled home an immaculate free-kick - and then scored another almost identical one!

STADIUM OF LIGHT

WE'RE GOING UP

SUNDERLAND AFC PROMOTION 2005

MATCH OF THE SEASON
Sunderland 2-1 Leicester City
Coca-Cola Championship · 23 April 2005

STADIUM OF LIGHT

JULIO SHOOTS FOR GOAL

CALDWELL AND LAWRENCE

60

He did get two goals and both were winners, so Bridges did play his part in a title-winning season, as he had in 1998-99 and back at Roker in 1995-96.

The 2004-05 campaign started badly. Just one win in the first five league games had McCarthy's men 17th as that Play-Off defeat looked like it had left a hang-over. As in the opening season at the Stadium of Light, the renaissance followed a reverse at Reading.

A Stewart hat-trick in a big win at Gillingham kick-started a run of four successive victories, climaxed by a Carl Robinson winner at Leeds, which lifted Sunderland into fourth place.

It took until November to climb a place higher and it wasn't until the last game of the calendar year that the Lads slipped into one of the automatic promotion positions for the first time. Defeat on New Year's Day at Preston made that move into second place a brief one, but Sunderland stubbornly stayed on the coat-tails of pace-setters, Wigan and Ipswich until over-hauling them with an eight-match winning run that took them to the top.

The final match of that sequence was a mid-week trip to title rivals Wigan, where as well as filling the normal away stand, the red and white army packed the big stand opposite the players tunnel too, meaning over half of the record-gate in excess of 20,000 were following the Lads. Reward came with a Marcus Stewart winner leaving promotion within touching distance. Goalkeeper Myhre left Sunderland in the mire, when he went off injured in the next game when Play-Off hopefuls Reading left the Stadium of Light with all three points, after sub Michael Ingham had replaced him. Later to win a cap for Northern Ireland, Ingham played in a 2-2 draw at promotion rivals Ipswich before manager McCarthy made the decision to promote young goalkeeper Ben Alnwick for a home game with Leicester which could secure a return to the Premier League.

Debutant Alnwick picked the ball out of his net after just five minutes, but kept his side in it with a great save from future Sunderland promotion-winner David Connolly. Goals from Stewart and Caldwell gave Sunderland the victory that meant promotion, once news came through that Ipswich had only drawn at Leeds, and Sunderland's place back in the Premier League was mathematically confirmed. It was the second time in four years news of an Ipswich result affected Sunderland's status.

Promotion duly secured, Sunderland showed they deserved to be top by coming from behind to clinch the title at a West Ham United desperate for points to reach the Play-offs. Carl Robinson signed-off the Stadium of Light season with a winner, this time against Stoke City on the day the Lads raised the Championship trophy.

MARCUS STEWART NETS THE WINNER AT WIGAN

...AND POST-MATCH CELEBRATIONS

COCA-COLA CHAMPIONSHIP 2004-05

	HOME						AWAY						
P	W	D	L	F	A	W	D	L	F	A	Pts	Pos
46	16	4	3	45	21	13	3	7	31	20	94	1st

FA Cup: 4th round, lost 0-3 at Everton.

League Cup: 2nd round, lost 2-4 on penalties after a 3-3 draw at Crewe Alexandra.

ATTENDANCES

Average (league): 28,817

Highest: 47,350 v Stoke City, 8 May 2005.

STADIUM **OF** LIGHT

63

GOAL OF THE SEASON
Stephen Elliott

Sunderland 1-3 Manchester United
Premier League · 15 October 2005

A curler into the top corner was no more than a consolation, but in such a season any consolation was gratefully welcomed.

If the 2002-03 season of 19 points was a terrible one, was the 2005-06 campaign worse? Within three seasons of setting the lowest-ever Premier League points tally, somehow Sunderland managed to set the bar even lower by collecting just 15 points.

And yet, the regular players in 2002-03 to a large extent are above criticism. Honest hard-working pro's such as Nyron Nosworthy, Danny Collins and Dean Whitehead bust a gut. It wasn't their fault they weren't good enough collectively. Players can only give their all and the fans recognised that. In tests of loyalty, this season was the supreme examination. Supporters could see that those tasked with playing were out of their depth, but the crowd stuck with them because they respected the effort.

At any level of football if you lose week-in week-out, heads go down, tensions appear and you end up on the wrong end of a good hiding, or even several good hidings. The fact that despite losing 29 of the 38 Premier League games, at no point did anyone beat them by more than three goals, tells its own tale. None of the regulars ever gave up and threw the towel in, although surely that must have been mentally tough.

Nine of those who played in the 5-1 defeat at Chelsea in the last match of the 20th season were full internationals. In contrast, of the eleven highest appearance makers in 2005-06, only four were full internationals, including Nyron Nosworthy who debuted for Jamaica six years later.

McCarthy had little to spend as he took his promotion winners into the top flight. At £1.8m, forward Jon Stead was his most expensive buy with seven figure sums also invested in another forward, Andy Gray and goalkeeper Kelvin Davis. Experienced top-level performers in Tommy Miller and Alan Stubbs were also acquired. Everton-man Stubbs signally failed to make the sort of contribution Steve Bould did when brought in as an accomplished old head at centre-back for a newly promoted team in 1999.

Things were so bad that no-one scored more than three goals in the league and four in total. In the cups, non-league Northwich Victoria genuinely fancied their chances at the Stadium of Light and though they were well-beaten 3-0, in the next round Sunderland lost to a team two divisions below them (Brentford) for the first time in almost 30 years. In the League Cup, extra-time was required to beat League Two Cheltenham by a single goal at home, before a very youthful Arsenal (including Seb Larsson) handed out a footballing lesson in winning 3-0.

Pre-season had culminated with an encouraging final warm-up match that produced a 1-0 win in Holland against AZ Alkmaar. A scrappy goal there from Miller provided hope that he would be able to contribute goals from midfield,

2005-06

PLAYER OF THE YEAR
Dean Whitehead

39+2 appearances · 4 goals

Dean won the official award with no-one receiving the Supporters' Association Award. On behalf of the players Whitehead made a presentation to the supporters for sticking with the players through the toughest of seasons.

STADIUM OF LIGHT

65

STADIUM **OF** LIGHT

A JUBILANT JULIO ARCA
CELEBRATES HIS STUNNING
FREE-KICK AT MIDDLESBROUGH

but the big plus was thought to be Kelvin Davis. Three spectacular saves and a clean sheet gave hope that, in what was going to be a hard season, at least Sunderland would have a good goalkeeper.

When the serious stuff started it took just eleven minutes for the warning signs to flash. Future Sunderland striker Darren Bent couldn't believe his luck as he bore down on Davis' goal only for the 'keeper to get his angles horribly wrong and leave the Charlton man with virtually an open goal to slot into. New man Gray would score, but would never do so again and a 3-1 defeat didn't augur well.

After five games there were still no points and only one goal - from on-loan forward Anthony le Tallec. Like Adnan Januzaj in 2016-17, le Tallec had talent, but seemed to want everyone else to do the graft.

Even when the first point arrived it was a disappointment. Going into a home game with West Brom, Sunderland had incredibly lost 20 Premier League games in a row (including their previous Premier season) and gone 25 without a win. Having led from the seventh minute through Gary Breen there was a feeling of inevitably when Albion equalised deep into injury-time through Zoltan Gera.

That long awaited victory was only a week away though as Miller struck and Arca floated home a beauty of a free kick as Sunderland stunned Middlesbrough on Teesside. Miller was on the mark again a week later as another point was gleaned at home to West Ham, but the upturn was short-lived. The only further point to come in the next 13 games was from a goalless draw at home to Bolton on Boxing Day.

By now, of course, Sunderland were cast miles adrift at the foot of the table. At least they kept battling, the last of that 13-game run seeing them go down by the odd goal in three at home to a Chelsea side en-route to retaining the title.

In the final table, second bottom West Brom would have twice as many points as Sunderland, but a second win of the season did come at the Hawthorns, courtesy of an own goal by former Newcastle man Steve Watson. It would be the second and final win in 37 Premier League games under Mick McCarthy. Only one more point would be accrued before the manager and the club parted ways with ten games left.

Sunderland turned to Kevin Ball as caretaker manager. Bally was, and is, Sunderland through and through. The best captain the club have had since the days of Charlie Hurley, Bally's task was to hold the fort and try and revitalise the team. Three more defeats indicated that, as when McCarthy had taken over, the die was cast, but at Everton on April Fools' Day, Sunderland were seriously unlucky to only draw on a day when Jon Stead finally broke his duck with his only goal of the season, albeit one almost as scrappy as the solitary Sunderland goal Danny Graham would score at the same ground nine years later.

DAVIS SAVES FROM BOLTON WANDERERS' EL HADJI DIOUF

For all his faults, Kelvin Davis had his good days too. At Manchester United all the pre-match talk was about how a win wasn't good enough for the Red Devils who were looking to give their goal difference a boost. While the match mathematically confirmed Sunderland's relegation the goalkeeper had a blinder as he helped Sunderland to the unlikeliest of goalless draws.

Davis was nicknamed 'Calamity Kelvin' for a reason though and illustrated why in the next game - the visit of Newcastle to the Stadium of Light. Fired up by Bally and a rare couple of good results, the Lads led after an hour in the derby, courtesy of on-loan Arsenal defender Justin Hoyte. Summing up his season, Davis was caught napping when future Sunderland man Michael Chopra scored his only top-flight goal for the Magpies, who went on to win at a stroll.

After Arsenal repeated their 3-0 league Cup score-line in the next home game, Sunderland still hadn't claimed a home league win after entertaining all the other 19 teams in the Premiership. However there was still one last chance. April had seen a home game with Fulham abandoned because of snow. This remains the only Premier League game anywhere abandoned due to the weather, but it served a purpose for Sunderland. Losing 0-1 when the original fixture was called off, when the re-arranged game was played at the end of the season somehow Sunderland finally pulled off a victory, local lad Chris Brown getting the winner.

When the campaign ended at Aston Villa the following weekend, a huge travelling army arrived with many of them in fancy dress. The end of an awful season was something to celebrate, but Sunderland would be back. Rumours abounded that the club was about to be taken over and a new chapter was due to begin.

PREMIER LEAGUE 2005-06

	HOME						AWAY						
P	W	D	L	F	A	W	D	L	F	A	Pts	Pos
38	1	4	14	12	37	2	2	15	14	32	15	20

FA Cup: 4th round, lost 1-2 at Brentford.

League Cup: 2nd round, lost 0-3 to Arsenal.

ATTENDANCES

Average (League): 33,904

Highest: 47,366 v Arsenal, League Cup Round 3, 25 October 2005

League highest: 44,003 v Arsenal, 1 May 2006.

MATCH OF THE SEASON

Sunderland 1-1 Tottenham Hotspur

Premier League · 12 February 2006

DARYL MURPHY'S 89TH MINUTE LEVELLER
AGAINST TOTTENHAM HOTSPUR

JUSTIN HOYTE

JON STEAD

STADIUM **OF** LIGHT

69

2006 07

NIALL THE MANAGER

As at the end of the 2016-17 season, rumours abounded during the summer of 2006 that the club was about to be taken over. Bob Murray was the club's longest-serving chairman. Barring a brief spell where he'd stepped down from the chair but remained as the biggest share-holder, while John Featherstone became chairman, Murray had been at the helm for 20 years.

History will judge him kindly. As chairman he had equipped the club with the Stadium of Light and the Academy of Light. Without Murray, Sunderland may well still be playing in a museum piece of a football ground and with third-rate training facilities. Undoubtedly, during his reign fans felt there should have been more invested in the team, but when he did release funds - such as to Terry Butcher in the summer of 1993 - Murray saw money wasted and preferred to invest in bricks and mortar.

Now 20 years after taking over from Sir Tom Cowie, with the club in free-fall, it was time for life-time Sunderland supporters Bob Murray and vice-chairman John Fickling to hand over the care of the club to someone else. The days when local millionaires could finance a successful football club had come to an end. TV money meant that the size of a club's fan-base mattered less in terms of finance. This was especially so at a club like Sunderland where the board's policy of affordable football meant big crowds, but relatively little in terms of gate receipts compared to clubs elsewhere, particularly in the more affluent south. To finance a football club in the years to come you needed to be a billionaire, and the North-East of England doesn't have too many of them. Sunderland would eventually attract a billionaire owner, but in the meantime the takeover was fronted by the ultimate front-man, Niall Quinn.

The former centre-forward spearheaded a group of mainly Irish businessmen known as the Drumaville Consortium. Local input came from the admirable head of Hays Travel, John Hays who was appointed vice-chairman with Quinn as chairman. When Niall was the fulcrum of a highly-successful team based on partnerships, his partnership with Kevin Phillips was the cutting edge. John Hays was, and is, red and white through and through - as are Bob Murray and John Fickling - but Niall's partnerships extended throughout the Drumaville team. It was Quinn who convinced them all to get involved, and that meant putting money into a club that had become the butt of the nation's jokes, but one which Niall knew could be the best place to be in football when you got things right.

During pre-season that year, Niall made the occasional appearance at the training base at the University of Bath, but was never seen without at least one phone to his ear.

PLAYER OF THE YEAR
Nyron Nosworthy
27+2 appearances · 0 goals
Nyron was a revelation at centre-back alongside Jonny Evans.

DAVID CONNOLLY WITH TOBIAS HYSEN AND DWIGHT YORKE AFTER SCORING THE FIRST FROM THE SPOT AGAINST DERBY

Lengthy negotiations were constantly underway confirming the consortium, arranging the finer points of the takeover ...and trying to get a manager.

Having stuck with the team through relegation before, only to subsequently suffer another dismal drop, crowd favourite Julio Arca knew it was time to move on. He also knew that he had to turn down Newcastle's advances or risk his love affair with the red and white army and openly asked if a move to Middlesbrough would upset the fans. Assured they would understand, Arca moved down the A19, but remained a cult hero in Sunderland where in 2017 he still lives, and works with youngsters at the academy.

Under the stewardship of coaches Kevin Richardson and Tim Carter, the Drumaville era kicked-off at Forest Green Rovers, as Quinn's quest for a manager continued. Eventually with pre-season preparation time running out, Niall stepped into the manager's role himself, appointing Bobby Saxton as first-team coach.

Four defeats in a row had Sunderland down with the dead-men. The fourth of those on a blisteringly hot day at Southend saw a glimmer of hope in the debut performance of sub Arnau, brought in from Barcelona's 'B' team. He was promoted into the starting XI for a midweek League Cup tie at Bury, the side propping up the entire Football League, after a start even worse than Sunderland's. As Niall took his seat in the Directors' box having come up from the tunnel he saw Arnau coming towards the tunnel and wondered if maybe the new signing needed a change of footwear? The news for Niall was that Arnau had been sent off. Sunderland duly lost 2-0 leaving 'the Mighty Quinn' to stride towards the post-match press pack. Not waiting to be asked anything before Niall announced that a 'world-class' figure would be appointed as manager within a few days.

That world-class figure was Roy Keane. Such a box-office name that Sunderland were rarely referred to in the media as anything other than 'Roy Keane's Sunderland'. Keane sat in the stands as Niall the manager bowed out with a 2-0 home win over West Brom. The attendance of 24,242 would be increased by over 20,000 more by the last home game of the campaign.

Once installed, Roy roared into the job as he would a tackle - full force. Appointed with a couple of days to go in the transfer window, half a dozen players arrived in the last few hours. Included amongst them was Stan Varga for a second spell at the club; having played with Roy at Celtic, and Dwight Yorke, persuaded to swap Australian beaches for shopping in Jacky White's market. You often hear of players not fancying the North-East. You don't often hear of players saying no to Roy Keane.

THE SCORER OF THE SECOND AGAINST THE RAMS LIAM MILLER IS CONGRATULATED BY JONNY EVANS

ROY KEANE

STADIUM OF LIGHT

STADIUM **O**F LIGHT

GOAL OF THE SEASON
Carlos Edwards
Sunderland 3-2 Burnley
Coca-Cola Championship · 27 April 2007

Fantastically fierce strike into the top corner for a winner that all but mathematically confirmed promotion.

MATCH OF THE SEASON
Sunderland 3-2 Burnley
Coca-Cola Championship · 27 April 2007

One man famous for saying 'No, no no' was Nyron Nosworthy, but not even 'Nugsy' said no to Roy. At the turn of the year Sunderland had climbed to just above mid-table when the manager used his Old Trafford connections to bring in young centre-back Jonny Evans. Right-back Nosworthy was told he was playing centre-back alongside him and was a revelation. Mick McCarthy - no shrinking violet himself - had previously asked Nyron to play in central defence, but the player hadn't fancied it. Put there by Keane the Nosworthy-Evans axis provided the base for a 17-match unbeaten run that zoomed Sunderland from mid-table to the top.

Keane didn't mess about. While Niall Quinn would later organise a fleet of taxis to get supporters home, Roy would leave players behind if they were late for the bus. On the other hand, on a later occasion during a pre-season in Dublin, Roy would instruct the team bus to pick up a little old lady at a bus stop in the pouring rain and give her a lift. Her friends probably still don't believe her tale, but that was Roy. At Sheffield Wednesday he went ballistic after a 4-2 win had massive away support booming 'Keano' to the tune of 'Hey Jude.' It was more 'Please Please Me' in the dressing room as he lambasted the team for giving two late goals away when they were four up, but the 'Long and Winding Road' of a 46-game season would have a 'Here Comes the Sun-derland' ending.

The 'Roy-volution' which had started with away wins at Derby and Leeds came down to a final home game with Burnley. It was one of the nights for which the Stadium of Light was built. Over the river, the Empire has seen some fine drama, just quarter of a mile away, Roker Park had many a fabulous fixture, but the Stadium of Light is home now and has been for two decades. It has a history of its own, a history for a new generation, a place where memories are forged alongside the Wear where dads and grandads made Sunderland the place it is. This night against Burnley was the sort of match that the children and grandchildren of the future will be told about.

The game ebbed and flowed. Former Sunderland striker Andy Gray scored at the Stadium of Light for the first time since his Sunderland debut. Top scorer that year David Connolly missed a crucial penalty and later took another one. Once converted, Connolly had no time for Stuart Pearce-style emotional release as at Euro 96. He just got the ball out of the net and raced back for the re-start. You can imagine how much Roy would have hated histrionics when there was a match to be won. When victory was delivered the winner was sent from the heavens. Wade Elliott had already scored as good a goal as a visiting team have ever scored at the Stadium of Light with a shot belted home from somewhere just outside of Whitburn, but Carlos Edwards' winner was even better.

Signed from Luton, Trinidadian Edwards had already mounted his own 'Goal of the Season' competition. He'd hit screamers

DAVID CONNOLLY CELEBRATES WINNING THE LEAGUE

ANTHONY STOKES GRABS THE FIRST OF FIVE AT LUTON

up and down the country, but he'd saved the best 'til last. As Daryl Murphy (who had also scored) laid the ball into his path attacking the north end, Edwards struck the ball as forcefully and as accurately as it is possible to hit a football. As the net won its award for bravery for not breaking, in the Directors' box Niall Quinn lurched forward out of his seat. The man who had eschewed the quiet life to come back to the club he'd played for and fallen in love with, the man who had used the most glittering of silver-tongues to talk a group of businessmen with largely no connection to Wearside to invest in a club that had been a bar-room joke, the man who had had to convince his wife Gillian that he hadn't lost his marbles, felt the weight of the world slide from his shoulders. The Magic Carpet ride had just taken a bend at 100mph and Sunderland were going up. Even Roy Keane skipped half a step and half-punched the air before stopping himself before anyone saw him!

As the 20th anniversary of the Stadium of Light is marked with Sunderland having just endured another depressing relegation, supporters and officials need to remember and understand that winning feeling, that promotion feeling. If the darkest hour comes right before the dawn then Carlos Edwards had just pulled back the curtains on the most beautiful of mornings.

In fact Sunderland still needed another result, but they were all but effectively up and when Derby lost at Palace two days later, even Roy Keane could afford a smile. There was one match to go, at Luton who were already down. Hatters fans made a killing selling their season tickets to Sunderland supporters who took over Kennilworth Road. There in the midst of it was Hertfordshire based Charlie Hurley - even 'the King' had come to the party.

The party had started the previous evening in nearby Northampton where Niall was on such form he karate-chopped a pile of 50 poppadoms in a local restaurant. At least it wasn't the Football League signs he was wrecking as at Bury in 1999. The Championship trophy was at Preston ready to be presented to Steve Bruce's Birmingham City but they slipped up as Sunderland strode to a 5-0 victory to take the Championship.

There would be no parade as for Roy Keane the thought of a club like Sunderland celebrating promotion was unseemly. Instead, a private ceremony took place at Seaham Hall. Nonetheless it had been a season of triumph as well as transformation. Sunderland were about to embark on their longest top-flight run since they lost their proud record of never playing anywhere but the top flight, in 1958.

COCA-COLA CHAMPIONSHIP 2006-07

	HOME						AWAY							
P	W	D	L	F	A	W	D	L	F	A	Pts	Pos
46	15	4	4	38	18	12	3	8	38	29	88	1st

FA Cup: 3rd round, lost 0-1 at Preston North End.

League Cup: 1st round, lost 0-2 at Bury.

ATTENDANCES

Average (league): 31,887

Highest: 44,448 v Burnley, 27 April 2007.

STADIUM OF LIGHT

2007·08

STADIUM **OF** LIGHT

GOAL OF THE SEASON

Andy Reid

Sunderland 2-1 West Ham United
Premier League · 29 March 2008

Technically a fine footballer, Andy Reid's 89th minute
North-End volley was a goal fit to win any game.

78

Promoted into the Premier League, Sunderland signalled their intent by breaking the British transfer record for a goalkeeper, rather than breaking it again as a seller, as they did following relegation in 2017. Costing £9m in 2007, Craig Gordon's arrival from Hearts showed that Sunderland were being backed by ambition as the Drumaville Consortium only had to build a team as Bob Murray had ensured the infra-structure was in place. It was like buying a house that was ready to move into rather than one that needed re-wiring. It was just a case of putting the decorations up.

Joining goalkeeper Gordon in debuting on a glorious day at home to Spurs were Kieran Richardson, Dickson Etuhu, Paul McShane and Michael Chopra, who came off the bench to score the winner with the only goal of the game in the last minute.

Not all of the early season debutants were successful. In the coming weeks Greg Halford, Roy O'Donovan, Russell Anderson and Danny Higginbotham would all make their bows, but it was the signing of centre-forward Kenwyne Jones who stirred the greatest excitement. He'd gone to the same school as Carlos Edwards in Trinidad, but he didn't have the same consistent commitment. If he was in the mood Kenwyne - or Ken-whine as a later teammate dubbed him - could be unplayable. He even had John Terry noting how tough he was to play against and when he scored, his trademark somersault celebration just added to the occasion.

However it was a season of struggle, of fighting for every point as the team tried to acclimatize to the higher level. For just under a month around the turn of the year Sunderland were in the bottom three, but generally they kept their heads above water, a run of three wins towards the end of March pretty much quashing any worries that were ended with a late Daryl Murphy winner in a 3-2 home win over Middlesbrough in the penultimate home game.

Despite a season of considerably more lows than highs and immediate elimination from both cups, crowds soared. There was a feeling that the club were looking up not down. There were clear leaders. Roy Keane was in his first managerial job, but had an aura of authority (although this proved to be his only full season as Sunderland manager). Behind the scenes chairman Niall Quinn was working on re-establishing a connection with the crowd that was as good as it had been for decades.

CRAIG GORDON

PLAYER OF THE YEAR
Kenwyne Jones
33 appearances · 7 goals

Kenwyne was top scorer with just seven goals, but his physical prowess made him a feared forward.

MARTON FULOP

Illustrating that such a connection doesn't depend on success - though that helps - it was a similar connection that Niall had witnessed as a player both for and against Sunderland.

In 1991, Niall scored twice for Manchester City as the Lads were relegated at Maine Road on a day when 14,000 away supporters gave their relegated heroes a breathtaking ovation. Managers often talk about the weight of expectation at Sunderland, but the only thing Sunderland supporters expect is effort. Give them that effort, as the 15-point team of a couple of seasons earlier had - and they'll stick with you. Fail to put in a shift and they'll find you out immediately - as some have found in more recent years.

In contrast with costly Craig Gordon making his debut on the opening day of the season at home to Spurs, on the final day it was the turn of another new goalkeeper to debut at the Stadium of Light, against Tottenham's north-London neighbours Arsenal.

The goalkeeper this time was former Spurs stopper Marton Fulop. A decent goalkeeper and a delightful bloke with a big smile, the Hungary international would sadly pass away at the young age of 32 in 2015. Goalkeeping coach Tim Carter who had helped Kevin Richardson as joint care-taker manager in the first few weeks of the Drumaville reign would also die tragically young. The loss of such people who have made such contributions to the early stages of the Stadium of Light story is something supporters won't forget.

PREMIER LEAGUE 2007-08

	HOME						AWAY						
P	W	D	L	F	A	W	D	L	F	A	Pts	Pos
38	9	3	7	23	21	2	3	14	13	38	39	15

FA Cup: 3rd round, lost 0-3 at home to Wigan Athletic.

League Cup: 2nd round, lost 0-3 at Luton Town.

ATTENDANCES

Average (League): 43,334

Highest: 47,802 v Arsenal, 11 May 2008.

DARYL MURPHY CELEBRATES THE THIRD GOAL

MATCH OF THE SEASON

Sunderland 3-2 Middlesbrough

Premier League · 26 April 2008

STADIUM OF LIGHT

STADIUM OF LIGHT

STEED MALBRANQUE CELEBRATES SCORING THE LADS' FIRST GOAL AT HULL CITY

Having been promoted three times in the opening decade of the Stadium of Light, 2008-09 was actually the second time the club's new home had to deal with the prospect of the infamously clichéd, but nonetheless worrying, 'second season syndrome'.

After the previous promotion, the team had gone straight back down with a bump whereas first time around Peter Reid's team had repeated their seventh place finish, an achievement which looks better with each passing year.

On this occasion, the season would be a struggle with manager Keane not lasting until Christmas. It would be a nervous edging over the line under Keane's successor Ricky Sbragia as Sunderland survived on 36 points, regardless of only taking one point from the last five games, and registering just a single victory in the final 13 fixtures. Finishing fifth from bottom, Sunderland were just four points ahead of bottom club West Brom. In a tight finish, they just managed to finish the right side as North-East rivals Newcastle and Middlesbrough went down.

Having barely conducted a transfer deal with Tottenham in the past, Sunderland suddenly decided to try and sign almost half their team: Steed Malbranque, Pascal Chimbonda and Teemu Tainio heading north, although Younes Kaboul thought better of it and declined a move he'd end up making seven years later. Following an opening day defeat at home to Liverpool, a win at White Hart Lane a week later helped towards a bright start which saw Sunderland sixth after five games. Further arrivals included El-Hadji Diouf, Djbril Cisse and Anton Ferdinand as Roy Keane evidently wasn't remotely bothered about the prospect of bringing big characters into the dressing room.

Ironically another 'new' face was the return of George McCartney from West Ham, Sunderland therefore managing to have paid the highest fee yet for a player produced by their own academy. Someone who would smash that record would be given his bow at the start of November when Jordan Henderson was used as a sub in a 5-0 defeat at Chelsea.

By then Sunderland had dropped to 16th, but the two wins they had managed since the trip to Spurs were a 2-0 home scoreline over 'Boro and even more importantly a 2-1 victory over Newcastle. The win over Newcastle ranks as one of the most memorable matches in the first 20 years of the Stadium of Light. A home win over the near neighbours was long overdue. While they had been beaten on several famous occasions at Newcastle, on Wearside the period of 28 years since their last loss was by far the longest the home support had gone without enjoying the victory which they savour most of all.

PLAYER OF THE YEAR
Danny Collins

41 appearances · 1 goal

Danny missed just three of the 44 league and cup games as he added the official Player of the Year award to the Supporters' Association Trophy he had won the year before and retained this time around.

83

Goals from Cisse and United's Shola Ameobi saw the teams go in level before the big moment came. Awarded a free-kick at the North End, Kieran Richardson stepped up to try and beat one-time Sunderland 'keeper Shay Given. A week earlier Richardson had been right out of luck with two dead-balls at Fulham. One had hit the woodwork and while the other found the back of the net the referee had ruled it out having spotted an infringement in the wall. This time though the heavens were with Kieran. He absolutely leathered the ball, connecting with it so perfectly that Given would have needed to watch 'Match of the Day' to see it. The frame of the netting lifted when the ball hit the rigging as the crowd erupted in the way that only a Sunderland crowd can erupt - especially after so long without a home win over the Magpies. It was Sunderland's day, victory didn't really look in doubt, only the margin of it, as the woodwork denied Cisse and Kenwyne Jones, but all that mattered was that the Stadium of Light had seen and enjoyed its first win over Newcastle.

On the day - and night - it was simply derby delight that concerned those of a red and white persuasion, but in the final analysis the wins over Newcastle and 'Boro were crucial in deciding which of the North-East's clubs would carry the region's flag into the Premier League for the following season.

Amazingly that win would be Roy Keane's last at the Stadium of Light. How football can quickly change. Regardless of his 'God-like status' in much of Ireland - something Sunderland staff and fans had seen for themselves in pre-season - you wouldn't have found an Irishman or woman with a higher opinion of him than Sunderland supporters that night - not even the Dublin lady on the bus!

Following the derby win, three defeats were followed by a second-half fightback which brought three points at Blackburn and lifted the team to eleventh, two games before Keane was sacked. A tame 0-1 home defeat preceded a home game with Bolton Wanderers where goalkeeper Craig Gordon was pressed into action having not played in six weeks. The Scot wasn't fit and was cruelly exposed by a Bolton side who helped themselves to four goals.

Having played for both Sir Alex Ferguson and Brian Clough there was no doubt which of them had influenced Keane the manager more. Roy regularly had a Brian Clough book or DvD to engage him and liked to talk about how Clough had been influenced by old Sunderland manager Alan Brown. Like Clough, Keane would often be conspicuous by his absence. If such an overpowering personality wasn't around the training ground it made a big difference. It was like the Rolling Stones without Mick Jagger, but evidently majority shareholder Ellis Short couldn't get any satisfaction out of a highly paid manager who didn't turn up often enough. With the Irish economy collapsing, the Drumaville investors had been looking for a way of bowing out of the 'Sund-Ireland' era.

MATCH OF THE SEASON
Sunderland 2-1 Newcastle United
Premier League · 25 October 2008

GOAL OF THE SEASON
Kieran Richardson

Sunderland 2-1 Newcastle United
Premier League · 25 October 2008

Richardson's rocket almost took the North Stand net off.
What a great goal to ensure, not only the first Wear-Tyne derby
victory at the Stadium of Light, but the first on Wearside in 28 years.

BELOW, EL HADJI DIOUF AND ANTON FERDINAND AT THE FINAL WHISTLE

STADIUM OF LIGHT

85

KIERAN RICHARDSON SCORES THE
FIRST PAST CHELSEA'S PETR CECH

20**08**09

STADIUM **OF** LIGHT

PREMIER LEAGUE 2008-09

		HOME						AWAY						
P	W	D	L	F	A	W	D	L	F	A	Pts	Pos
38	6	3	10	21	25	3	6	10	13	29	36	16th

FA Cup: 4th round, lost a replay 2-1 after extra-time at Blackburn Rovers.

League Cup: 4th round, lost 1-2 at home to Blackburn.

ATTENDANCES

Average (league): 40,168

Highest: 47,936 v Newcastle United, 25 October 2008.

Irish-American Ellis Short had become the majority shareholder in the month before the win over Newcastle, having acquired a 30% stake.

Keane's view was that 'less was more' and he had more impact by turning up when it mattered most, as Clough had done. Additionally, in this modern era of mobile phones it wasn't as if Roy was cut off, and in terms of watching opponents and transfer targets he appeared to be as diligent as any manager. After all, Keane had been the player who chose to miss out on a World Cup because of what he perceived as less than professional preparation. Whatever the rights and wrongs of the situation Roy was removed a week before a trip to Manchester United by which time coach Ricky Sbragia was in charge.

A narrow defeat at Old Trafford was followed by 4-0 and 4-1 wins with Sbragia persuaded to drop the caretaker bit of the caretaker-manager title after a Boxing Day draw at home to Blackburn that left the Lads in a reasonably healthy 14th place at the season's half-way point.

A decent little run in February saw Sbragia's Sunderland slink up to tenth place, but a 1-0 home win over lowly Hull would be the only maximum return from the last 13 games as Sbragia took only two thirds as many points from the final 15 fixtures that Keane had from the first 15 prior to his dismissal.

Portsmouth is the home of HMS Victory, but one eluded Sunderland there in midweek of the final week of the season when safety was in sight. Instead on the morning of the final day of the campaign, WBA were already down, 'Boro were as good as down and needed a miracle to stay up and it would be one of Sunderland, Newcastle or Hull to join them.

With two wins in seven months, Hull were at home to the Red Devils who had already tied up the title, Newcastle were at Martin O'Neill's Aston Villa and Sunderland were due to entertain third placed Chelsea. Future Sunderland man Darron Gibson gave United an early lead with what would prove to be the only goal at Hull, to take the pressure off somewhat, as Sunderland embarked on what would be defeat by the odd goal in five to Chelsea. Meanwhile at Villa Park a first-half own goal by Damian Duff would result in Newcastle joining Middlesbrough in going down. This left Hull and Sunderland safe, to cue scenes of wild celebration at the Stadium of Light. Rarely, if ever, can a defeat have been treated with such glee, but before the personnel had left the ground, manager Sbragia stepped down, relieved to be out of the hot-seat, leaving Sunderland once again looking for a new direction.

That direction was signposted three days after the final game when it was announced that having now gained 100% of the club, Ellis Short had become the first-ever sole owner of Sunderland AFC.

NIALL QUINN AND ELLIS SHORT

RICKY SBRAGIA

STEVE BRUCE

LORIK CANA

Oddly, the most enduring image of this season is that of a beach-ball. It was a case of 'Oh we do like to be beside the seaside' as the beach-ball got the final touch to the only goal of a 1-0 home win over Liverpool. That shouldn't disguise that fact that it was a fourth successive home victory and the previous one had seen Sunderland score five.

There were certainly good days under new manager Steve Bruce. Raised a Newcastle supporter, there were plenty of doubts about his appointment, and many of them were from Steve himself. He was concerned as to whether he would be accepted. Re-assured by the sight of the statue of Bob Stokoe, Steve understood that if his results were good, no-one would bat an eyelid about his boyhood loyalties.

Having only had novice managers since the departure of Mick McCarthy, 'Brucie' had been around the block and knew what was involved in running a club. He was closely involved in incoming transfers, in particular convincing Darren Bent to come and score goals for Sunderland. Scoring goals was something Steve knew required an array of forwards and he made sure he got them. Partnering Bent with Kenwyne Jones, Bruce also brought in Frazier Campbell and by his second season, having lost patience with Jones, he'd added to his fire-power, giving him a choice of Bent, Campbell, Asamoah Gyan and Danny Welbeck.

In his first season though, Sunderland revolved around Bent who got 24 in the Premier League and another against Premier League opposition in the cup. Jones contributed nine and Campbell chipped in with four, although no-one else scored more than twice.

Bruce also re-energised central midfield, bringing in Lee Cattermole, who he had previously signed for Wigan, along with Albania captain Lorik Cana, signed from Marseille. The two of them took no prisoners and before injury disrupted their partnership after the 'beach-ball' win over Liverpool in October, Sunderland had settled into seventh place in the Premier League and were looking like a more than decent team. That run of four home wins had seen nine goals scored in the middle two and while away form wasn't great a 2-2 draw at Manchester United augured well for the future.

Another Bent strike earned a home win over Arsenal which kept Sunderland eighth as November ended. The value of taking 20 points from the first 13 games was illustrated by the fact that a mid-season slump that brought no further wins in 14 games, only dropped the team by six places.

PLAYER OF THE YEAR

Darren Bent

40+1 appearances · 25 goals

Darren was never the most popular player at the Stadium of Light following his sudden transfer mid-way through the following season, but in 2009-10, his 24 Premier League (and one cup) goals were more than Jermain Defoe managed in either of his full seasons at the club.

STADIUM OF LIGHT

89

2009-10

GOAL OF THE SEASON
Bolo Zenden

Sunderland 3-1 Tottenham Hotspur
Premier League · 3 April 2010

One of the most spectacular goals ever seen at the Stadium of Light, Bolo Zenden's top-class technique was never better seen than with an acrobatic volley that sealed victory in what had been a superb match.

MATCH OF THE SEASON

Sunderland 3-1 Tottenham Hotspur
Premier League · 3 April 2010

FRAIZER CAMPBELL AND DARREN BENT

That poor run was emphatically ended as Bent bagged a hat-trick in a 4-0 home win over Bolton. It was one of nine home wins enjoyed by the Stadium of Light crowd with a late season win over Spurs also seeing two missed penalties as well as the three goals Sunderland did score, Bolo Zenden's 'goal of the season' being far more worthy of memory than Bent's beach-ball goal.

At the Stadium of Light, Sunderland were pretty good. Only three games were lost and nine won in the league and a tally of 13 goals more scored at home than conceded was a figure bettered only by the top eight. On the road though, things were tougher. Only one game was won following the opening day victory with all but five of the 18 trips that followed the victory at Bolton being fruitless journeys.

Despite such highlights the 2009-10 season doesn't live in the memory quite as much as some other campaigns because what it lacked was nail-biting drama. Sunderland finished 14 points clear of the third bottom side, neatly positioned in 13th place. It was the highest top-flight points tally since the start of the decade and under Bruce the club had detached themselves from the sides threatened with relegation.

In the final analysis there was a comfortable five-point gap to the team immediately beneath them in 14th place and in turn fully 14 points, plus a vastly better goal difference between SAFC and the drop zone. Consequently, there was reason for optimism that funded by Ellis Short the second decade of the century would see Sunderland edge further up the table.

PREMIER LEAGUE 2009-10

	HOME					AWAY							
P	W	D	L	F	A	W	D	L	F	A	Pts	Pos
38	9	7	3	32	19	2	4	13	16	37	44	13th

FA Cup: 4th round, lost 1-2 at Portsmouth.

League Cup: 4th round, lost 1-3 on penalties after a 0-0 draw at home to Aston Villa.

ATTENDANCES

Average (League): 40,355

Highest: 47,641 v Manchester United, 2 May 2010.

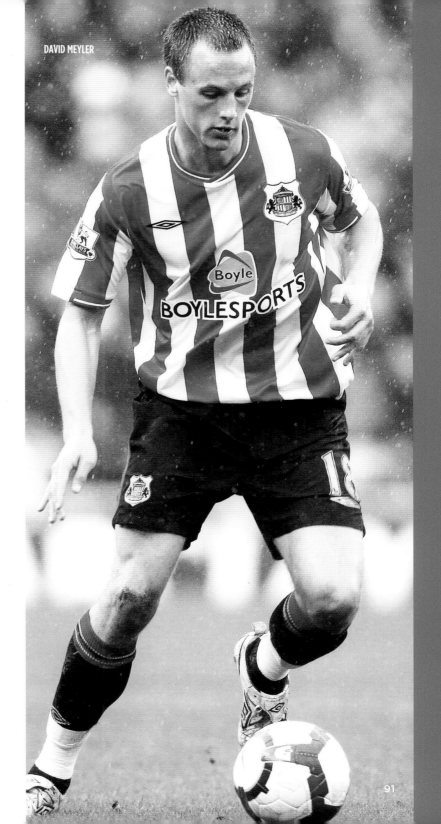

DAVID MEYLER

91

CRISTIAN RIVEROS

Sunderland spent the second decade of the Stadium of Light entirely in the top flight. In that period they managed just one top-half finish. It came when a final fixture win at already relegated West Ham lifted the Lads three places from where they started the day.

It was a tight middle of the table. Had Sunderland lost that last game they would have been 14th. One more win and they'd have been eighth - just a place behind the best at the Stadium of Light.

Under Steve Bruce they spent three months from mid-November to mid-February in either sixth or seventh position. The season was derailed by Darren Bent's departure. Going into the Stadium of Light derby in mid-January, Sunderland sat sixth after the only back-to-back Premier League wins of the campaign. A packed crowd anticipated a good chance of a home win, but Bent didn't look himself and it was the man brought in to complement him, Asamoah Gyan, who got Sunderland's goal in a disappointing 1-1 draw. Shortly afterwards came news that Bent wanted away, with a record-breaking deal to Villa worth up to £24m soon following.

Things had been going very well under Steve Bruce. His first season had seen Sunderland finish in an encouraging 13th place - three places and eight points better off than the season before he arrived. This 2010-11 campaign would see another three place and three-point climb despite Bent's departure, but had Bent stayed surely there would have been an even bigger lift as Bruce built his team.

Things turned sour for Steve the following season, but undoubtedly he had the nous to assemble a squad good enough to cope with the big league and the man-management skills to get the best out of people. His time at Sunderland can be looked at rather like the Alan Durban era in the early eighties, when a good team was being put together only for the potential not to be fulfilled.

The season began with a 2-2 draw at home to one of Bruce's old teams, Birmingham. Summer investment meant there were half-a-dozen debuts. Paraguay international midfielder Cristian Riveros had been signed before the World Cup finals in which he had scored. Centre-half Titus Bramble re-joined Bruce having played for him before at Wigan, Ahmed Elmohamady arrived from Egypt and would do well enough for Bruce that he would later take him to Hull, while a loan each from the Manchester clubs brought in Nedum Onuoha and Danny Welbeck. Best of all was goalkeeper Simon Mignolet, signed for a bargain couple of million from Belgian club St. Truiden.

ASAMOAH GYAN SLOTS
HOME THE SECOND

2010·11

MATCH OF THE SEASON

Chelsea 0-3 Sunderland

Premier League · 14 November 2010

Best SoL game, Sunderland 4-2 Wigan,
Premier League, 23 April 2011

NEDUM ONUOHA CELEBRATES SCORING THE FIRST GOAL

THE SCORER OF THE THIRD, DANNY WELBECK

STADIUM OF LIGHT

93

STADIUM OF LIGHT

GOAL OF THE SEASON

Jordan Henderson

Sunderland 4-2 Wigan Athletic
Premier League · 23 April 2011

Future England captain Jordan Henderson scored twice in this game, one of them the result of a mazy dribble completed with a fierce shot lashed into the North Stand net.

94

GYAN AND BENT

Amongst the departures were two big names. Captain Lorik Cana returned from pre-season with the shock announcement that he wanted to leave, while Bruce's exasperation with Kenwyne Jones reached breaking point in the final pre-season friendly at Hoffenheim. On his day Jones could be unplayable, but Bruce had higher ambitions than players who could turn it on when they felt like it. He wanted characters who he knew what he was going to get from them, and with young Welbeck completing an attacking quartet including Bent, Gyan and Campbell he had other options up front.

The first win of the season was in what proved to be the first of four consecutive 1-0 home wins over moneybags Manchester City, a penalty from Bent in the third game following a 1-0 loss at West Brom. Five successive draws included good ones against Arsenal, Liverpool and Manchester United before a home win over Aston Villa lifted Sunderland up to seventh ahead of the derby at St. James.'

Sunderland were favourites going into the big day and had a great chance to take an early lead only for Welbeck to fire into the side-netting when he should have squared it. It turned into a disaster as Newcastle won 5-1, appropriately enough on Halloween. It was an awful day for everyone connected with the club. Excluding days on which relegations have been confirmed, it was probably the worst in the twenty years since moving to the Stadium of Light. To Steve Bruce's credit, unlike many a manager who has hidden in the dug-out when things have been going badly, but been keen to be seen when things have gone well, Steve stoically stood in the technical area throughout and took every last bit of stick that came his way. What's more, he made a point of wearing his Sunderland tracksuit rather than a suit that day. Following his departure he lost some respect from fans due to his thoughts on how his Newcastle background hindered his time on Wearside, but when he was at the club, Steve Bruce did a better job than most in actually putting a team on the pitch.

In the recent past, good derby results had sparked positive runs. In this case the manager and players responded in style, Gyan in particular hitting form. The Ghana international got two goals in a home win over Stoke and one at White Hart Lane where Spurs were held to a draw. The best was to come in the third match after the derby. Travelling to a dominant Chelsea who had done the double the year before, Sunderland excelled. While Chelsea have undoubtedly had the upper hand against Sunderland in the modern era, Sunderland have saved some of their best performances for games against them and this was one of them.

The previous year had seen the Blues inflict a 7-2 defeat on Sunderland at Stamford Bridge with left-back Ashley Cole running riot. Bruce detailed versatile left-back Kieran Richardson to play on the right-wing and pin Cole back.

PLAYER OF THE YEAR
Phil Bardsley

34+3 appearances · 3 goals

Phil was used as a sub just once in the first five games, but once he got in the side, he was never left out. Solid in either full-back berth he also notched three goals.

JORDAN HENDERSON

The plan worked as well as any plan could and was summed up in the last minute when Richardson's pressing forced Cole into an ill-advised back pass that led to Welbeck's first goal for the club. Amazingly it completed a 3-0 score-line. Nedum Onuoah had waltzed through the home defence for a brilliant individual opener before Gyan continued his scoring spree with the second.

Never the shy and retiring type Gyan's celebratory dance provided one of the great comedy moments when Bolo Zenden - normally so smooth and sophisticated - joined in with some dad dancing he's lived to regret ever since. Great days, the sort of occasion that makes up for the bad days. Sunderland could not have made a better response to the desperate derby other than by beating Newcastle.

While Gyan got Sunderland's goal in the return derby that ended all square, Bent's departure made it another dismal day. Once again Richardson's versatility proved invaluable as in the next match his move into an advanced role brought him both goals in a 2-1 win at Blackpool that kept Sunderland sixth. With money re-invested in Stephane Sessegnon it was hoped Sunderland could survive the loss of the man who bagged more goals per season than anyone other than SuperKev since the Stadium of Light opened. They couldn't.

Only one point was taken from the next nine games, and that from a goalless draw. Gyan scored a couple in that run, but Sessegnon didn't get on the scoresheet until converting a penalty on the day the winless run ended. It needed to, as Sunderland were starting to look over their shoulders having dropped to 15th place with five games to go.

Busy making his name as a local lad with a great engine and no little talent, Jordan Henderson got a couple of important goals as six second-half goals brought a 4-2 win over lowly Wigan to life. It was the first of three wins in the last five matches of the season as Sunderland ended the campaign on the up.

Henderson however had caught the eye of other clubs and was to lead the list of departures in the summer, a reported fee in the region of £16m taking him to Liverpool. Bent never emulated his Sunderland success elsewhere while Henderson has gone on to be one of the top stars in the country. Ultimately Bent's transfer arguably wasn't the biggest loss from the squad, but unlike Bent, Henderson is always assured of a warm welcome whenever he returns to the Stadium of Light.

PREMIER LEAGUE 2010-11

		HOME					AWAY						
P	W	D	L	F	A	W	D	L	F	A	Pts	Pos
38	7	5	7	25	27	5	6	8	20	29	47	10th

FA Cup: 3rd round, lost 1-2 at home to Notts County.

League Cup: 3rd round, lost 1-2 at home to West Ham United.

ATTENDANCES

Average (league): 40,011

Highest: 47,864 v Newcastle United, 16 January 2011.

STEPHANE SESSEGNON NETS AGAINST WOLVES AT THE STADIUM OF LIGHT

STADIUM OF LIGHT

2011 12

STADIUM OF LIGHT

SEBASTIAN LARSSON EQUALISES AGAINST LIVERPOOL WITH A STUNNING VOLLEY

Jordan Henderson was involved in SAFC's first game of the season at Anfield. Unfortunately, it was for Liverpool following his transfer, but there were Black Cats debuts for Wes Brown, Ji Dong-won, David Vaughan and Seb Larsson, who scored Sunderland's goal in a 1-1 draw with an acrobatic volley.

John O'Shea, Keiren Westwood, Connor Wickham, Craig Gardner and Nicklas Bendtner were others to make their bow in the opening weeks, as yet again there was a churn of players, so prevalent in the modern game. Largely gone are the days where a team would stay together and so Sunderland once more had a new look as they looked to continue building on the progress of the past two seasons.

The big issue would be having a regular scorer. Kevin Phillips, Darren Bent and Jermain Defoe have been the best strikers in the Stadium of Light era, but 2011-12 was one of those years where the absence of a regular goal-scorer was the missing link in an otherwise decent side.

Bendtner top-scored with eight Premier League goals, but was reminiscent of Kenwyne Jones in that he could be excellent or anonymous. To the credit of the team as a whole, the same number of goals were scored as in the season before and there were only three fewer than the year before that when Bent bagged 24.

Much of the play was shaped around the inventiveness of Sessegnon who got seven with Larsson equalling that tally from four fewer appearances. The Swede's dead-ball prowess was to the fore as he moved towards one of two notable club records. Larsson has scored more free-kicks than anyone in the club's history and also would overtake the great Charlie Hurley as Sunderland's most capped international.

While Sunderland dropped three places to 13th from the previous year's tenth, they actually improved their goal difference by ten goals having tightened their defence. This was despite a series of injuries constantly disrupting the centre of defence, where Brown showed his class in the first half of the season before being crocked in the second when Michael Turner became the main man after returning from injury.

It was a season of managerial as well as team changes. While there was a good early 4-0 home win over Stoke, it was the only victory in the first seven games, leaving Sunderland just one place above the dreaded bottom three.

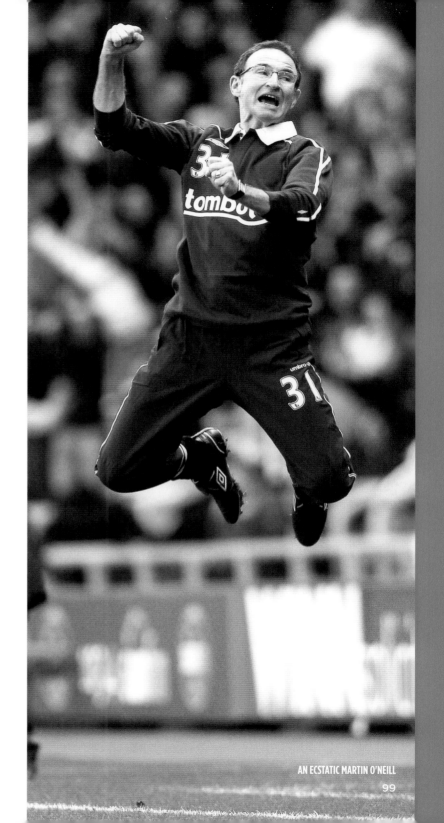

AN ECSTATIC MARTIN O'NEILL

SIMON MIGNOLET

JI DONG-WON

MATCH OF THE SEASON

Sunderland 1-0 Manchester City

Premier League · 1 January 2012

City dominated throughout but couldn't beat 'man in the mask' Mignolet. When Ji Dong-won kept his balance to beat Joe Hart with the only goal of the game in the last minute City probably felt all of the Sunderland side should have worn masks. It was a stunning victory after a determined rear-guard action inspired by a brave goalkeeper.

By mid-November there had only been one more win with Sunderland in 16th place after what proved to be Bruce's last stand, a 1-2 home defeat to his former club Wigan when the atmosphere turned vitriolic.

It was only November, but desperate for a win, Bruce took left-back Bardsley off for midfielder Vaughan and six minutes from time right-back O'Shea made way for forward Dong-won. Instead of 'respecting the point' as Big Sam Allardyce would have said in years to come, Bruce felt pressurised to get all three and ended up with none, almost inevitably Sunderland got hit on the break in the last minute.

Having sacked Bruce four days later, Sunderland installed Eric Black as caretaker manager for a defeat at Wolves by which time new boss Martin O'Neill was already sat in the stands. Having traded a boyhood Newcastle supporter in Bruce for a boyhood Sunderland fan in O'Neill, there could be no prospect of the gaffer's background causing him any grief and O'Neill got off to a tremendous start.

Two late goals, from Vaughan and a Larsson free-kick turned defeat into victory against Blackburn. This set Sunderland off on a run of seven wins and a draw from ten games with the only defeats being 1-0 scorelines at Spurs and Chelsea.

By the end of this sequence Sunderland had jumped from 17th to eighth with O'Neill celebrating the last of those wins at the home of vanquished manager Tony Pulis after snow stopped him returning to his own home. Sunderland had just won 1-0 at Stoke where the only goal of the game came from young Irish winger James McClean.

Brought in by Bruce at the start of the season along with ex-Arsenal youngster Roarie Deacon, the pair were seen as ones for the future, but O'Neill took one look at McClean in the reserves and gave him a debut in his own first match. The winger was a revelation at first, but would fall out big-time with Sunderland supporters in subsequent years for non-footballing reasons.

Nonetheless, McClean was part of the red and white revival, one of his five goals coming in a 3-1 home win over QPR that kept Sunderland eighth in the last week of March. It took Sunderland to 40 points from 30 games, but there would be just five draws and no more wins from the final eight games as Sunderland settled into a final spot of 13th.

Knowing when to leave the stage has always been the preserve of masters of their profession. The Beatles never did get back together after breaking up just eight years after their first big hit. John Cleese never would make

GOAL OF THE SEASON
Ji Dong-won

Sunderland 1-0 Manchester City
Premier League · 1 January 2012

A good goal, but not the greatest, as the South Korea international stumbled before applying the finishing touch, but for pure drama this last minute winner goes down as one of the Stadium of Light's greatest moments.

20 11-12

STADIUM OF LIGHT

NICKLAS BENDTNER SCORES FROM THE SPOT

DAVID VAUGHAN

JAMES McCLEAN

102

another series of 'Fawlty Towers' and Niall Quinn had hung up his boots after one game of the Howard Wilkinson regime. Niall knew when to go. Having handed over the baton as chairman of the club to Ellis Short in October, Niall had continued as Director of International Development. With Sunderland in the top half of the Premier League and with an FA Cup quarter-final to come, the club from the Stadium of Light were light years away from the club he took over just as they had been relegated with a measly 15 points.

Quinn had always made it known that he would be back at the club for a period of between five and ten years. This was his sixth season back at Sunderland. Having played, managed and chaired the club, having pulled together a consortium to take over when SAFC was at a horribly low point, Niall Quinn had made his mark.

Charlie Hurley from Cork had been the club's first Player of the Century and Niall Quinn has set down a benchmark for the club's man of its second century to also be an Irishman. Declining the suggestion of a statue or a stand named after him, Quinny was happy to have the Stadium of Light Sports Bar re-named in his honour and sank the first pint of Guinness pulled there after its re-branding. One thing for certain is that whenever he's back, Niall will never be short of someone wanting to buy him a pint - or pay for his taxi home.

PREMIER LEAGUE 2011-12

		HOME					AWAY					
P	W	D	L	F	A	W	D	L	F	A	Pts	Pos
38	7	7	5	26	17	4	5	10	19	29	45	13th

FA Cup: 6th round, lost 0-2 at home in a replay to David Moyes' Everton.

League Cup: 2nd round, lost 0-1 after extra-time at Brighton & Hove Albion.

ATTENDANCES

Average (League): 39,095

Highest: 47,751 v Newcastle United, 20 August 2011.

PLAYER OF THE YEAR
Stephane Sessegnon

42 appearances · 8 goals

Flashes of skill in tight situations always endeared the Benin international to the crowd. He missed only two league games and scored a cup winner at Middlesbrough.

DANNY ROSE GETTING THE BETTER OF SERGIO AGUERO

20 12 13

MATCH OF THE SEASON

Sunderland 1-0 Manchester City

Premier League · 26 December 2012

The 3-0 win at Newcastle rightly tops this match, the third of four successive 1-0 home wins over City was the pick of the games at the SoL.

STADIUM OF LIGHT

With the only league defeat by the end of October being away to Manchester City, it would be reasonable to expect a higher position at that point than 14th. However with the only win having been a 1-0 home result against Wigan the table didn't lie.

The other half-dozen Premier League matches had been drawn. These included a decent point from a first-day goalless draw at Arsenal, a home 1-1 against Liverpool and the same score-line at home to Newcastle, thanks to a late own goal from Demba Ba.

What rankled with manager Martin O'Neill was the postponement of the opening home game with Reading due to a water-logged pitch - in August. O'Neill maintained that three points from that early game would have had a positive psychological effect on players and fans as in an embryonic table early points made a big difference. He had a point. On the morning of the derby for example, had Sunderland played and won that Reading game they'd have gone into the match above Newcastle rather than below them. Ifs, buts and maybes don't count of course and Sunderland had to get on with it.

By the time the re-arranged match with Reading came around Sunderland did win, 3-0. It was a result that helped O'Neill to the December Manager of the Month award. Back-to-back wins at Southampton and at home to Manchester City either side of Christmas made for a good festive period. After a solid start though, there were too many bad days as Sunderland slipped briefly into a relegation position before the game in hand was won.

January provided the opportunity for strengthening, but the signings of Alfred N'Diaye, Kader Mangane and Danny Graham failed to ignite a spark in the side. When one of the summer's big signings, Steven Fletcher, was injured playing for Scotland in March, it dealt a blow to Sunderland's survival chances.

O'Neill's own survival chances ran out following a home defeat with Manchester United at the end of the month in which his main striker Fletcher had been injured. As the 'Party with Marty' reached closing time, only three points had been taken from the last eight games as Sunderland sat marooned in 16th place.

If there had been a party with Marty (there hadn't - it was serious stuff to the studious O'Neill) any prospect of the high jinks continuing, ceased when disciplinarian Paolo Di Canio was appointed as Head Coach.

Vesuvius itself might as well have erupted, such was the furore over the Italian's appointment. Reports of Sunderland's new leader's alleged fascist salutes and Mussolini tattoo overwhelmed the club for a while.

Many supporters withdrew their backing and the Durham Miners' Association decided to remove their Monkwearmouth Lodge Banner, which has pride of place on one of the main

GOAL OF THE SEASON
Seb Larsson

Sunderland 3-0 West Ham United
Premier League · 12 January 2013

A spectacular left-foot volley from distance helped in a decisive victory over West Ham.

PLAYER OF THE YEAR

Stephane Sessegnon

39 appearances · 7 goals

The playmaker retained the award and showed his versatility by starting the season in the 'hole' under Martin O'Neill and then operating on the right and finally as a striker under Paolo Di Canio. Goalkeeper Simon Mignolet was the North East Football Writers' Player of the Year for the region.

staircases at the Stadium of Light. The banner is almost an umbilical cord connecting the past with the present. It links the previous generations of Sunderland supporters with those of the modern day. Preserving that link is essential for contemporary crowds to take heart from the club's heritage. Thankfully, the miners were persuaded to keep the banner there for the benefit of the supporters, but the fact its removal had even been mooted was indicative of the depth of feeling.

Di Canio began with a narrow defeat from a tough test at Chelsea, before facing up to Newcastle at St. James'. It was the sort of fixture Paolo relished and set in train, a record breaking six successive wins over the Magpies. Sunderland didn't just beat Newcastle, they hammered them on their own patch with three stunningly spectacular goals. Whatever the non- footballing objections to Di Canio, there was no getting away from the fact that he lived and breathed football. If Niall Quinn had disco pants, Paolo had dirty ones as he produced a knee-slide of Olympic qualifying proportions in his goal celebrations. He absolutely lapped it up, as did the suspended Craig Gardner who watched the match in the away end.

Ecstatic at the result, Di Canio attributed victory to seeing the face of his dead mother Pierina before the kick-off, a year and a day on from her death. Di Canio believed this gave him energy and anything that he felt took energy away from his players, was banned, including ketchup!

Welcomed for his first home game like a returning hero after leading the charge at Newcastle, Paolo was on the pitch conducting the crowd at the end of his first home game, after overseeing a 1-0 win over Everton.

That would be as good as it got for Di Canio or Sunderland that season as a 6-1 thrashing at Aston Villa brought everyone down to earth. Two more home draws helped the Lads over the line to an eventual 17th place finish - a place lower than they had been when O'Neill was sacked.

PREMIER LEAGUE 2012-13

	HOME						AWAY						
P	W	D	L	F	A	W	D	L	F	A	Pts	Pos
38	5	8	6	20	19	4	4	11	21	35	39	17th

FA Cup: 3rd round, lost 0-2 at home in a replay to Bolton Wanderers.

League Cup: 4th round, lost 0-1 at home to Middlesbrough.

ATTENDANCES

Average (League): 40,544

Highest: 47,456 v Newcastle United, 21 October 2012.

TOUCHLINE CELEBRATIONS
AFTER DAVID VAUGHAN'S
THIRD GOAL FOR THE LADS

STADIUM OF LIGHT

CONNOR WICKHAM HAMMERS THE
SECOND GOAL AT THE ETIHAD STADIUM

201314

STADIUM OF LIGHT

SUNDERLAND A.F.C.

108

Rarely, if ever, can a season of so many defeats have had so many highs. Sunderland lost 20 league games including eleven at home and yet a glance at the 'Match of the Season' section illustrates how many big days there were in the calendar and the 'short-list' for the Match of the Season doesn't even include them all.

Amazingly after a season down among the dead-men, Sunderland finished 14th. When you consider that they also reached the final of one cup and the quarter-final of another, it looks on the surface as if it was a good season, but during the slog of defeat after defeat, it didn't seem like it for most of the time.

Gus Poyet arrived as Head Coach during in the autumn and later decreed that a miracle was needed to keep Sunderland up. This is the club where a 'Messiah' did win a cup at Wembley and while Poyet didn't reach Stokoe's stature, the ride on the 'Gus-Bus' was like a drive down the Amalfi coast - on the edge, but with serious thrills - particularly when Connor Wickham took over in the driver's seat.

It was Italian international Emanuele Giaccherini who got the Premier League revival under way. Six weeks after Sunderland had put up a terrific, but ultimately fruitless show against all-conquering Manchester City in the Capital One Cup final at Wembley, the Lads turned up at City looking down and out. The game was a re-arranged fixture after the original fixture three weeks before the Wembley show-piece was postponed around an hour before kick-off ,due to high winds and in the intervening period Sunderland looked to have been blown away in the league.

Sunderland arrived at the Etihad on the back of five defeats, including a 5-1 collapse at Spurs in the previous away game. Rooted to the bottom of the table, seven points from safety with six games left, it did indeed need a miracle. City, Chelsea and Manchester United were all still to play away. Having beaten Sunderland in the Capital One Cup final, City were en-route to taking the league title too and had scored nine goals in their last two home games. When Sunderland fell a goal behind in the second minute it looked bleak, but the Black Cats clawed their way back into the match. Twice Giaccherini set up Wickham to put Sunderland astonishingly in front seven minutes from time. Failing to hang on, when Mannone let his old Arsenal clubmate Samir Nasri's shot slip through his fingers with two minutes remaining, could have deflated any hope of staying up, having got so close to a precious and unexpected win. Instead Sunderland went to Chelsea three days later and promptly ended Jose Mourinho's proud 77 game unbeaten home league record with the Blues, Wickham

BOTH SCORERS AT CHELSEA, CONNOR WICKHAM AND FABIO BORINI

CHELSEA'S MARK SCHWARZER IS BEATEN BY BORINI'S SPOT-KICK

scoring again after once more Poyet's team fell behind early on. It was the first time since 1933 that Sunderland had won a top flight game away to a top two side after going a goal behind.

Sunderland were still bottom of the table after four points out of nowhere, but now filled with confidence, a 4-2 win over fellow strugglers Cardiff lifted Sunderland out of the bottom three with Wickham scoring twice and winning a penalty. The miracle continued back where it began, in Manchester, when having won at Old Trafford on penalties earlier in the year after losing 1-2 on the night - Sunderland produced a first league win at Manchester United in 46 years. This time Wickham turned provider, teeing up Seb Larsson for the only goal of the game. Despite those final three trips being to the two Manchester clubs and Chelsea, somehow Sunderland had been unbeaten in their final three top-flight away games for the first time since 1952.

Amazingly when West Brom came to the Stadium of Light, a 2-0 win made it four wins in a row and after being seven points behind with six games to play, suddenly Sunderland were safe with a game to spare. Sunderland have had many late dates with destiny, but as far as great escapes go, this one warranted its description as the Greatest Escape.

The season had actually started with a cup final defeat at the hands of Manchester City, losing to an Edin Dzeko goal in Hong Kong in the final of the Barclays Asia Trophy. Hopes were high after Cabral and David Moberg-Karlsson were amongst the scorers as Spurs were beaten 3-1 in the semi-final in Asia. That duo were part of a 14-strong gaggle of signings brought in by new Director of Football Roberto De Fanti, who was appointed in June 2013 along with Valentino Angeloni, the pair having worked on behalf of Inter and Udinese.

At the time, the powers that be at SAFC felt that the new scouting system and Director of Football model would be the way forward and would pave the way to a scenario whereby if the Head Coach changed, the replacement would continue with the same group of players brought in by the Director of Football. It didn't work. De Fanti was sacked by January 2014 with signings such as Valentin Roberge, Modibo Diakite, Andrea Dossena, and Charis Mavrias joining Cabral and Moberg-Karlsson in having short-lived and unsuccessful sojourns at Sunderland.

Paolo Di Canio was sacked five league games into the season, having accrued a single point at Southampton where Sunderland led for 86 minutes, courtesy of a goal from one of the better buys, the diminutive Giaccherini. The Italy international needed time to settle in England, but did possess ability and a work ethic. Di Canio departed after a bad defeat at West Brom where the fans turned on him when he came onto The Hawthorns pitch to indicate they needed to keep their chins up.

SEBASTIAN LARSSON ON TARGET AT OLD TRAFFORD

GOAL OF THE SEASON
Fabio Borini

Sunderland 2-1 Newcastle United
Premier League · 27 October 2013

Having taken one point from the first eight games, Fabio Borini's 86th minute North End screamer not only registered the second of the 'six in a row' derby wins. It also got new head coach Gus Poyet a vital win in his first home match.

MATCH OF THE SEASON

Sunderland 2-1 Newcastle United

Premier League · 27 October 2013

There were probably more outstanding matches than in any year since the Stadium of Light opened: The Capital One Cup final, both legs of the semi, the quarter-final win over Chelsea and ending Mourinho's unbeaten home league record at Stamford Bridge, but maybe none of those would have happened without the dramatic home derby win that ended a dreadful start - oh and there was another 3-0 win as the double was done over the Magpies!

STEVEN FLETCHER

Once again Kevin Ball took over the reins in the short term, steering the club to a Capital One Cup win and two spirited, but fruitless performances in home defeats by Liverpool and Manchester United.

Sunderland turned to Uruguayan Gus Poyet. He had scored for Chelsea in one of the Stadium of Light's best-ever games when Sunderland scored four in the first half, back in 1999. There were four goals in a half in his first game as Head Coach, but they all went in at the wrong end as a second-half collapse at Swansea featured two own goals.

As with Di Canio, Poyet's second match was a derby, but a home one. Having scored at the wrong end at Swansea, Steven Fletcher struck with an early goal and while Mathieu Debuchy levelled for the Tynesiders, the Stadium of Light was to witness one of its moments of high drama when one of De Fanti's men came up with a moment that would have shook the Colosseum, Borini smashing home a truly great goal from outside the box with just a few minutes remaining.

The first league win lifted the team off the bottom of the table and the next home league game saw another 1-0 win over Manchester City. In between, cup progress had continued, victory over Southampton meaning there had been three home cup wins under three different head coaches.

There had also been a defeat at Hull where injury to 'keeper Keiren Westwood had seen another Italian acquisition come on for his debut. Vito Mannone was to establish himself as first choice and illustrate that for all the failures of the De Fanti shopping spree, there were some successes.

Mannone's greatest moments were to come in the cup. By the time the two-legged semi-final with David Moyes' Manchester United was to come around, Sunderland had started to adapt to Poyet's passing game. They were stringing together some decent results, but were still rooted to the bottom of the table despite one defeat in seven games in all competitions.

The Stadium of Light hadn't staged a major cup semi-final since its second season when defeat was tasted to Martin O'Neill's Leicester, but this time an own goal from Ryan Giggs and a Borini penalty gave Sunderland a 2-1 advantage to take into the second-leg. It was proving to be an excellent cup run, extra-time having been needed to knock out Chelsea at home.

As confidence grew, Sunderland began to play with some style and a sell-out 8,558 followed the Lads to Manchester for the second-leg of the semi. Former Sunderland loanee Jonny Evans scored the only goal of the 90 minutes to take the tie into extra-time. With a minute left, one-time United right-back Phil Bardsley struck a shot that squirmed through David de Gea, but when Javier Hernandez equalised in injury time of extra-time there was still more drama to come. It wasn't the greatest of shoot-outs as only three were scored, but try

PLAYER OF THE YEAR
Vito Mannone

35+1 appearances · 0 goals

The Italian goalkeeper spent his 26th birthday at Wembley playing in the cup final he'd helped Sunderland reach having been the hero of the semi-final penalty shoot-out.

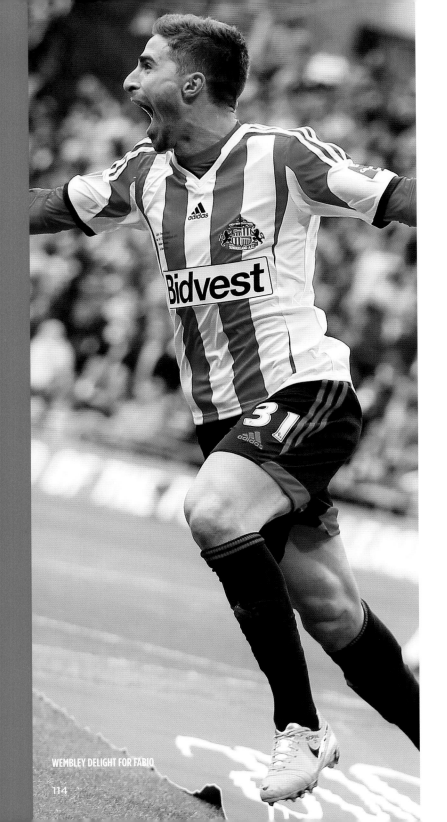

telling that to Mannone who saved from Adnan Januzaj and Rafael while Danny Welbeck and Phil Jones missed the target. On a night to remember, Sunderland's shoot-out successes came from loan men Ki Sung-Yueng and Marcos Alonso.

The following league game saw Sunderland climb out of the bottom three for the first time since August after a 1-0 home win over Stoke, before the dizzy heights of 14th were briefly attained after Newcastle were totally outplayed on their own pitch as Sunderland won 3-0 for the second successive visit.

Borini held his nerve to open the scoring from the spot in the derby and it was Borini again with a shot across future Sunderland 'keeper Costel Pantilimon who put Sunderland 1-0 up at Wembley in the Capital One Cup final at the beginning of March. Thousands had 'Dared to Dream' in Covent Garden the night before, but sadly unlike '73, there wasn't to be a happy ending as City came back to win, a last minute goal in a 3-1 defeat being harsh on Sunderland who produced a performance to be proud of.

That performance wasn't matched a week later by the tamest of FA Cup exits at Hull, having reached the quarter-finals, leaving the quest for cup glory gone in a flash, but the battle for Premier League safety still to win. A tame home nil-nil with Crystal Palace followed by five defeats made it look like Sunderland would emulate the only other season they had reached the League Cup final. That had been accompanied by relegation in 1985, but then came that night back at cup final opponents Manchester City and the Greatest of Escapes.

'Miracles do happen Gus' as a banner of the time informed the previously despondent head coach. Managers and head coaches come and go, but the fans have seen it all, and 2013-14 was a season full of the sort of drama Sunderland and the Stadium of Light are renowned for.

PREMIER LEAGUE 2013-14

	HOME					AWAY						
P	W	D	L	F	A	W	D	L	F	A	Pts	Pos
38	5	3	11	21	27	5	5	9	20	33	38	14th

FA Cup: Quarter-final, lost 0-3 at Hull City.

League Cup: Final, lost 1-3 to Manchester City at Wembley.

ATTENDANCES

Average (League): 41,090

Highest: 46,313 v Newcastle United, 27 October 2013.

20**13**14

BORINI FROM TWELVE YARDS AGAIN AT ST. JAMES' PARK

KI SUNG-YUENG

GUS POYET AT THE FULL-TIME WHISTLE AT NEWCASTLE

SEBASTIAN LARSSON SCORING FROM A FREE-KICK AT HOME TO EVERTON
AND BELOW, DEFOE, BRIDCUTT AND LARSSON CELEBRATE A 2-0 VICTORY
AT THE END OF THE REVERSE FIXTURE AT GOODISON

PLAYER OF THE YEAR
Seb Larsson

39+1 appearances · 3 goals

The Sweden international's contribution was recognised as he missed just two games in straining every sinew for the cause.

STADIUM OF LIGHT

DANNY GRAHAM CELEBRATES WITH PATRICK VAN AANHOLT AFTER SCORING THE BLACK CATS' OPENER AT EVERTON

Sunderland have reduced all of their supporters to tears at some point, be they tears of joy, relief or despair. In the 18th season of the Stadium of Light, Sunderland brought two of the most experienced men in the game to tears. Neither Jermain Defoe nor Dick Advocaat had any previous connection to the North East and neither of them were even at the club at the start of the season, but by the end of yet another dramatic campaign, both of them had shown that it is far from just Niall Quinn for whom Sunderland got under their skin!

JD's tears came as he celebrated scoring one of the greatest goals of his illustrious career to win the fifth derby in a row against Newcastle. Advocaat was overcome with emotion after a goalless draw at Arsenal secured Sunderland's place at the top table. It left a man who had won leagues and cups in three countries, won two European trophies and managed six national teams realising that Sunderland had a special magic all of its own.

The season started with five of the first six league games drawn, with a 1-0 loss at QPR matched by a home win over Stoke. While Sunderland had to wait until the seventh league game for that first three-point haul, it meant the team were in a decent enough 12th place going into the October international break.

Sunderland scored three goals in their next game. The trouble was they were all own-goals as the club record-defeat of 8-0 was equalled at Southampton. Although Arsenal would win at the Stadium of Light a week later, the draws kept coming, so that just before Christmas, ten of the 16 league games had finished all square, with two wins and four defeats before victory at Newcastle saw Sunderland settled in 14th place at Christmas.

Under Gus Poyet, the passing game was not what the paying public were used to or particularly wanted. While results were reasonable, no-one was particularly complaining, they were just bored. Supporters were not craving 'up and at 'em' route one tactics', the crowd knew what Poyet's philosophy was and there was respect for him sticking to it, but afternoons at the match on freezing cold winter days didn't provide much to warm to, other than in a spirited home goalless draw with Chelsea.

With Lee Congerton now in the Director of Football role, the big signing had been Jack Rodwell. Other new faces included Patrick van Aanholt and a winger Poyet had been eager to bring from his former club Brighton, Will Buckley.

JACK RODWELL CELEBRATES SCORING ON HIS RETURN TO MANCHESTER CITY

117

MATCH OF THE SEASON

Sunderland 1-0 Newcastle United

Premier League · 5 April 2015

He was re-united with his old Seagulls teammate Liam Bridcutt who Poyet had signed in the first transfer window after his arrival.

However, undoubtedly the signing of the season and indeed one of the best signings Sunderland have made in the Stadium of Light era was the January acquisition of Defoe. Many thought of him as an ex-England striker, but such was JD's impact, that he forced himself into the England set-up during his time at Sunderland. In 2017 he would even become the first Sunderland player to score for England at Wembley since the man the Stadium of Light Visitor Centre was named after when the stadium was being built: Len Shackleton.

What made Defoe's signing even more inspired is that he came in a swap deal from Toronto for USA international Jozy Altidore, who had been an expensive misfit since joining from Dutch football in 2013, after he had impressed with AZ. Defoe took 34 minutes of his home league debut to score - thereby equalling Altidore's tally in his 42 league appearances for the club (The American added a couple more in cup ties).

By the time Defoe scored his next Stadium of Light goal against Newcastle, Poyet had gone. A run of seven games without a win leading up to the Gus Bus reaching its terminus included a home defeat to rock-bottom QPR, previously without a point in a dozen away trips. There was also a tame cup elimination at League One Bradford City and a home game with Aston Villa where Sunderland were four down at half-time at home for the first time since 1958.

With nine games to play, only four of which were at the Stadium of Light, Dutchman Dick Advocaat was turned to, following Poyet's dismissal with the Lads hovering one place above the drop zone.

Advocaat was top drawer. He exuded confidence and belief. Whether talking to his players or staff behind the scenes the Dutchman's man-management was such that everybody was determined to do their best for him. It is a default position in any football club for people to want to try and impress the Gaffer, but for Advocaat they went the 'extra-mile' - in the players' cases probably literally as they ran their hearts out for him.

There was an improvement in defensive organisation immediately as Advocaat began away to Big Sam Allardyce's West Ham where a late goal denied Sunderland a point. A week later, who should be Advocaat's first opponents at the Stadium of Light, but Newcastle United, making him the third Sunderland boss in a row to have a second game - and a first win against the Magpies. Defoe detonated the day with one of the all-time great derby goals that brought his tears. Dick's were not far off.

GOAL OF THE SEASON
Jermain Defoe

**Sunderland 1-0 Newcastle United
Premier League · 5 April 2015**

Given the quality of the strike and the importance of the game, perhaps only Carlos Edwards' goal against Burnley in 2007, SuperKev's stunner against Chelsea in 1999 or Richardson's Rocket in 2008, also against the Magpies, can rival this as the goal of the first 20 years at the SoL. The superb 22-yard left-footed volley at the South Stand had Londoner Defoe in tears as the enormity of scoring in the Wear-Tyne derby hit him.

STADIUM **O**F LIGHT

STADIUM OF LIGHT

JORDI GOMEZ SCORES PENALTY NUMBER TWO AT HOME TO THE SAINTS

He might have felt like crying in his second home match when - as in Poyet's last - four goals were let in at home, an eleven-minute Yannick Bolasie hat-trick doing the damage as Crystal Palace won 4-1. Advocaat analysed the loss, and the Lads would not lose again until after they were mathematically secure.

A draw at Stoke was followed by the only back-to-back league wins of the campaign. Two Jordi Gomez penalties brought some sort of revenge over Southampton before Defoe added to Danny Graham's solitary Sunderland goal in a tremendous 2-0 win at Everton.

Sunderland were left with three games to save their skins. With trips to Arsenal and Chelsea to complete the season a home game with relegation threatened Leicester was one the Lads needed to win. The Foxes were completing their own great escape though and having got the point they needed left Sunderland looking down the barrel with the Stadium of Light's fixtures over.

Everyone else in the Premier League had one game to play. Sunderland and Arsenal had a game in hand and each needed the points. The Gunners wanted victory to assure themselves of third place and keep alive hopes of runners-up spot. At the other end of the table, with QPR and Burnley doomed, Sunderland required a point to stay up and leave Hull and Newcastle to squabble over the third relegation slot.

In stark contrast to the defence who had conceded eight at Southampton or four three times at home, Sunderland were an organised unit at the Emirates. Costel Pantilimon had one of his best games for the club, behind a side who defended with heads and hearts while managing to make some presentable chances of their own. One point was sufficient and as Advocaat and his men saluted the magnificent Red and White Army, both he and his assistant of 25 years, Bert van Lingen, were reduced to tears as they saw for themselves what the result meant to the fans.

These were men used to managing teams who won leagues and cups. There was no trophy for them for guiding Sunderland to safety, but there was a memory indelibly stamped upon them. When the season came to a close the following weekend at Stamford Bridge where Chelsea received the Premiership trophy there were no blues for Sunderland. It had not been a season with as many highs or lows as the year before, but the tears of Dick and Defoe showed it had been yet another chapter in the Sunderland story that had stretched the emotions of even the most experienced of characters.

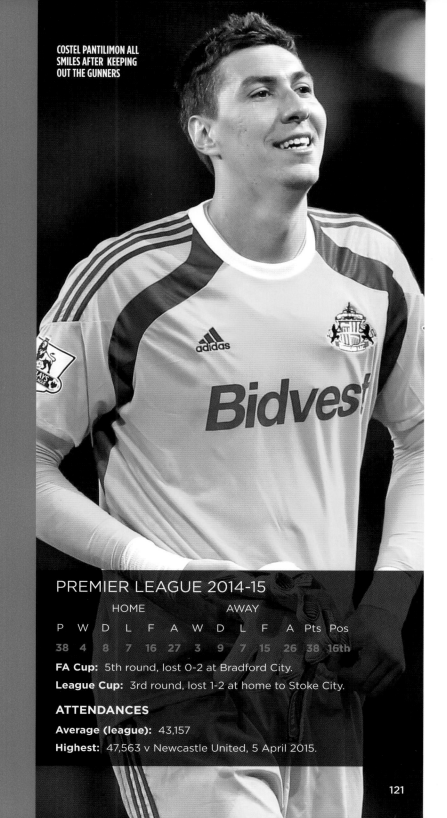

COSTEL PANTILIMON ALL SMILES AFTER KEEPING OUT THE GUNNERS

PREMIER LEAGUE 2014-15

	HOME					AWAY						
P	W	D	L	F	A	W	D	L	F	A	Pts	Pos
38	4	8	7	16	27	3	9	7	15	26	38	16th

FA Cup: 5th round, lost 0-2 at Bradford City.

League Cup: 3rd round, lost 1-2 at home to Stoke City.

ATTENDANCES

Average (league): 43,157

Highest: 47,563 v Newcastle United, 5 April 2015.

121

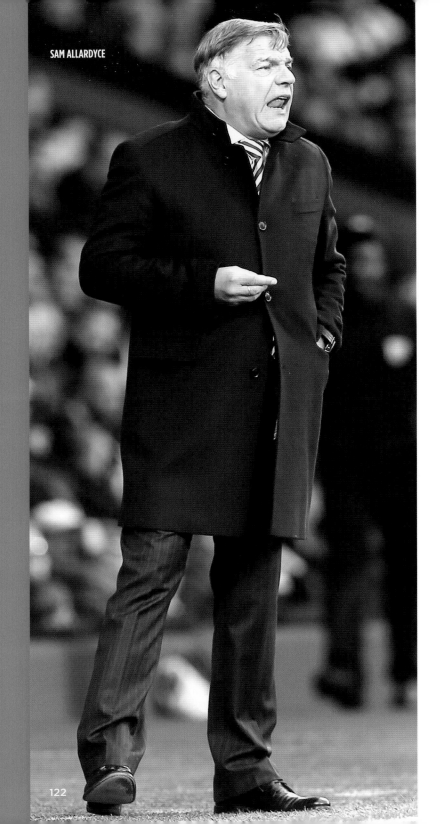

SAM ALLARDYCE

Flowers sent by fans to Dick Advocaat's wife helped persuade the Dutchman to change his mind and return, after deciding to call it a day following the previous season's escape act.

Within half-an-hour of the new season he might have wished he'd just found enough tulips in Amsterdam for Mrs A himself. By then, Sunderland were three down, albeit at Leicester who were about to have season their fans might only have previously been able to dream about had they frequented the coffee houses of old Amsterdam.

Adam Matthews came off the bench at Leicester to become Sunderland's 1,000th player, but it would be the only league appearance of the season for the Wales international brought in by Director of Football Lee Congerton. Other new faces included Jeremain Lens and Ola Toivonen who had played for Advocaat before, Younes Kaboul, Yann M'Vila who played more games than anyone, and soon DeAndre Yedlin on loan from Spurs. There was also the return of Fabio Borini, signed at the end of the transfer window, a year on from his heroics while on loan from Liverpool.

As in the opening season of the Stadium of Light, an early home defeat by Norwich contributed to a bad start. Goals from M'Vila and Lens in a draw at Aston Villa, who would prop up the table, produced one of only three points gleaned from the opening nine games. Lens was on the mark again with a goal of genuine class, tarnished by a red card as the third of those points was won at home to West Ham, after which Dick decided he'd been right to leave in the first place and resigned, feeling he could take the team no further.

Whereas Advocaat had been Head Coach; as had Poyet and Di Canio, his replacement, Sam Allardyce, was appointed as manager. Sunderland lost to a scruffy goal at West Brom in Allardyce's first game, but as with his three predecessors, Big Sam was to find that the sight of Newcastle United coming next on the fixture list was to be a blessing. By now, used to losing derby matches, the Magpies were swept aside at the Stadium of Light. They were walloped for the third 3-0, in what was the sixth in the 'six in a row' run. This one though, was at the Stadium of Light and, as always, a derby victory put right a lot of wrongs in lifting the crowd's spirits.

Six wasn't such a popular number at Everton a week later as Sunderland lost 6-2 as they experimented with a three at the back system. When this was followed by a 0-1 home reverse to Southampton, the Lads had just six points from 12 games and were looking a long way from safety. Back-to-back wins at Palace and at home to Stoke propelled the team briefly out of the bottom three, but the year ended with five defeats in a row leaving Sunderland 19th at the turn of the year, seven points behind fourth bottom Swansea with half the fixtures played.

2015 16

PLAYER OF THE YEAR
Jermain Defoe

29+5 appearances · 18 goals

JD's 15 Premier League goals were a major factor in keeping Sunderland up. His haul included a hat-trick at Swansea. He also took home a match ball from the Stadium of Light having scored three in a 6-3 League Cup win over Exeter City.

STADIUM OF LIGHT

LAMINE KONE'S HEADER LED TO THE WINNER AGAINST MANCHESTER UNITED

124

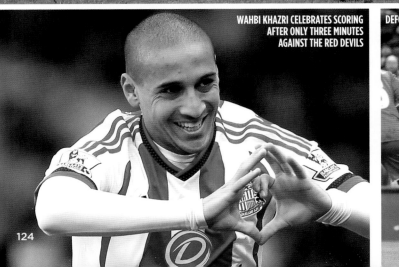

WAHBI KHAZRI CELEBRATES SCORING AFTER ONLY THREE MINUTES AGAINST THE RED DEVILS

DEFOE EQUALISES TWO MINUTES FROM TIME AT ANFIELD

While Sunderland were still 19th when January ended, it was to be one of the best and most important months in the club's recent history. So often transfer windows have seen signings be disappointing to say the least, but in January 2016, Big Sam knew where the bargains were. Rather like when you see Aldi have won a gold medal for their champagne, Allardyce bought quality at bargain prices. Lamine Kone, Jan Kirchhoff and Wahbi Khazri weren't household names when they arrived. Hardly a Sunderland supporter would have heard of them until they were about to sign, but by the end of the season each of them had more than repaid their transfer fees with a series of performances that made mincemeat of the arguments that overseas players must have time to settle into the English game.

Key to the settling in of Kone and Khazri, who came from French football, was Younes Kaboul. Behind the scenes his importance in helping them fit in was as important as Emerson Thome's had been when Julio Arca joined.

Improvement began before the newcomers arrived as Jermain Defoe struck five goals in the first two league games of 2016, a brace helping to see off back-markers Villa on Wearside before a hat-trick in a 4-2 victory at Swansea. Sunderland then led at Spurs before being thrashed 4-1, after Kirchhoff came off the bench for a desperate debut that saw him concede a penalty and deflect a goal beyond Jordan Pickford who was making his Premier League bow. Pickford had first appeared a week earlier at Spurs' rivals Arsenal in the FA Cup.

Kone and Khazri's debuts would coincide with Kirchhoff's first start at the beginning of February in a narrow home defeat by Manchester City. It was a night where against top opponents, Sunderland upped their game and with the newcomers impressing, people could see Big Sam was getting the side into shape, with another new face, Dame N'Doye also debuting as a late sub.

Two late goals at Anfield earned an unlikely point against Liverpool where the home fans walked out early in a pricing protest, but Sunderland were good value for victory in the next home match as Manchester United were beaten thanks to a Khazri free-kick and a Kone header that was too much for David de Gea.

Sunderland though, were still 19th and stayed there after defeat on Allardyce's return to West Ham. It was Sunderland's final game at the Boleyn Ground as the Hammers prepared to move to the Olympic Stadium, almost two decades on from when Sunderland moved to the Stadium of Light.

'Respect the point' was Big Sam's mantra and a series of four draws kept the points tally ticking over, one of them at Newcastle seeing the six in a row run end, but extending the unbeaten derby run to nine.

JAN KIRCHHOFF

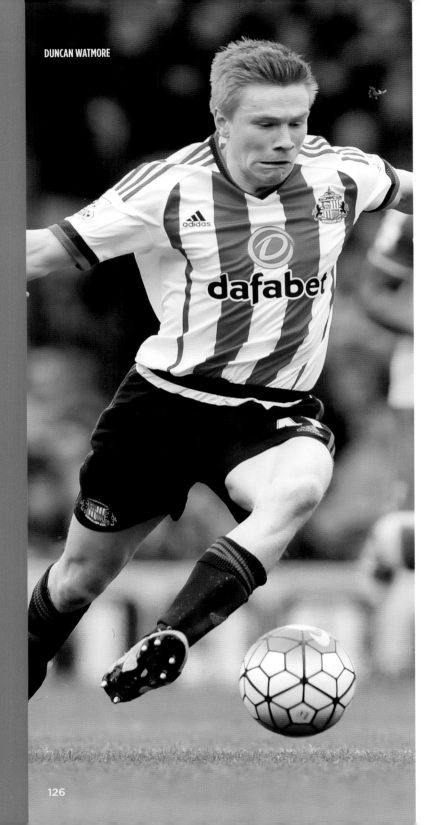
DUNCAN WATMORE

Having started their season in dreamland with victory over Sunderland, champions elect Leicester won on Wearside, but it was to be the only defeat in Allardyce's last eleven games. Still in a relegation spot after the Foxes stole the points, Sunderland finished with three wins and three draws as another great escape was completed. A magnificent 3-0 win at relegation rivals Norwich was followed up with a battling point from a home goalless draw with Arsenal, before a final-minute penalty by Defoe added another point at Stoke.

The final two home games of the season were two of the finest seen in the history of the Stadium of Light. The atmosphere in victories over Chelsea and Everton were the Roker Roar re-incarnate. Against Chelsea, Sunderland won a top-flight game after twice coming from behind for the first time since 1966. It was a humdinger of a match, a goal of the season-volley from Khazri cancelling out Diego Costa's opener. Nemanja Matic restored the lead for the visitors only for two goals in three minutes from former Blue Borini and that man Defoe to turn the game - and indeed the season - on its head. Few had expected Sunderland to beat the Blues while results elsewhere went Sunderland's way, leaving the Black Cats to leap out of the bottom three with a week of the season to go.

As in the previous season, Sunderland had a game in hand in the final week. This time it was at home and more records were broken as Kone became the first central-defender to score more than once in a top-flight game for Sunderland since 1903 as Everton were brushed aside 3-0. Victory secured safety with a game to spare, condemning Newcastle and Norwich to the drop on an euphoric night that sent the crowd home happy and full of optimism for the season to come.

PREMIER LEAGUE 2015-16

	HOME					AWAY						
P	W	D	L	F	A	W	D	L	F	A	Pts	Pos
38	6	6	7	23	20	3	6	10	25	42	39	17th

FA Cup: 3rd round, lost 1-3 at Arsenal.

League Cup: 3rd round, lost 1-4 at home to Manchester City.

ATTENDANCES

Average (League): 43,071

Highest: 47,653 v Newcastle United, 25 October 2015.

GOAL OF THE SEASON

Wahbi Khazri

Sunderland 3-2 Chelsea
Premier League · 7 May 2016

So often the goal of the season contributes to a game becoming the match of the season and this one certainly did. The Tunisia international's volley screamed into the South Stand net, a goal that was as spectacular as it was important.

MATCH OF THE SEASON

Sunderland 3-2 Chelsea

Premier League · 7 May 2016

BORINI GETS THE LEVELLER

...AND DEFOE THE WINNER

STADIUM **O**F LIGHT

2016/17

PLAYER OF THE YEAR
Jermain Defoe

38+2 appearances · 15 goals

Defoe's consistency brought him 15 Premier League goals. It was the first time a Sunderland player had managed as many as 15 goals in successive top flight seasons since Charlie 'Cannonball' Fleming in the mid-fifties. Defoe's goals got him back into the England team, where he became the first man since Fleming's 'Bank of England Team' colleague Len Shackleton to score for England at Wembley while on Sunderland's books.

GOAL OF THE SEASON
Jermain Defoe

Sunderland 3-0 Hull City
Premier League · 19 November 2016

As with his 'Goal of the Season' against Newcastle two years earlier J.D.'s goals could be measured for their quality as well as their quantity. This one in the same South Stand goal as his howitzer v Newcastle came at the end of a twisting run, and was his 150th in the Premier League.

Not since the halcyon days of Quinn and Phillips had supporters looked forward to a season in more buoyant mood. The momentum of the previous campaign, where the only defeat in the last eleven games was to the champions, had been maintained.

Efforts by Everton to prise away dominant defender Lamine Kone for a reported £18m had been resisted. The side had a spine of a solid centre-half, a striker who would score regularly and get into the England team and a young home-grown goalkeeper in Jordan Pickford, who once brought in would also get into the England team, and come the end of the season would be sold for a British record fee for a goalkeeper, worth up to £30m. To complete that spine, Sunderland would shortly invest £13m in midfielder Didier Ndong, having decided not to acquire the previous season's stalwart Yann M'Vila for £8m, the stated aim being to bring him in for free in January.

As fans turned up for the opening friendly at Hartlepool however, the PA had good reason to be playing 'Three Lions'. Sam Allardyce was imminently about to be appointed manager of England, leaving Sunderland to recruit yet another leader at a time when 'strong and stable' leadership was about to become something the nation would be told it needed.

Newly appointed Chief Executive Martin Bain secured the popular appointment of the experienced David Moyes. He was a big name long-craved by Sunderland and was warmly welcomed by the fans in a pre-season fixture at Rotherham when he was unveiled as the new manager.

As well as Ndong, the new boss brought in over a team's worth of new players. Centre-back Papy Djilobodji arrived for a reported £8m from Chelsea, youngsters Paddy McNair and Donald Love came from Manchester United, from whom Sunderland also acquired Adnan Januzaj on loan. Januzaj's fellow Belgium international Jason Denayer joined on loan from Manchester City, as did full-back Javier Manquillo from Atletico Madrid. As the season progressed, former Evertonians Steven Pienaar, Victor Anichebe, Joleon Lescott, Bryan Oviedo and Darron Gibson came in. Additionally, goalkeeper Mika Domingues was recruited after Vito Mannone became one of many players to go down with long-term injury.

Departures included Younes Kaboul after the first game of the season and Patrick van Aanholt who rejoined Allardyce at Crystal Palace in January, after Big Sam's brief flirtation with the national team. A stunning 4-0 away win over Allardyce's new side in February was a rare highlight for Sunderland in what became a sorry season.

Making the worst start in Premier League history; taking only two points from the first ten games, left Sunderland with a range of mountains to climb, not just one. From very early on in the campaign, manager Moyes was forthright in his honesty about how difficult he thought the challenge would be.

DAVID MOYES

DIDIER NDONG

JORDAN PICKFORD

The introduction of Anichebe brought brief respite as his three goals in two games propelled the team to the season's only back-to-back wins, at Bournemouth and at home to Hull. Watching the Hull match were Charlie Hurley and his 1964 promotion-team, on the day The Charlie Hurley Centre gates were sited outside the stadium. It was a day on which the lights went out at the Stadium of Light, but thankfully were restored within eight minutes as the staff behind the scenes helped to ensure a rare day of success.

Reigning champions Leicester were beaten the following month in the best home performance of the campaign. A fortnight later, a third home win of the season would prove to be the last victory home fans would witness, with Christmas not yet reached. Never out of the bottom three from September, Sunderland propped up the table from February onwards and finished 17 points from safety, manager Moyes resigning a day after the season ended.

Throughout the year, terminally-ill young supporter Bradley Lowery captured everyone's hearts, particularly Jermain Defoe's. The bond between the pair was genuine, just as the bond between the crowd as a whole and the club and all it stands for, is a deep and genuine one. Brilliant Bradley provided a sense of perspective when fans contemplated the lows of football.

As the 20th season at the Stadium of Light came to an end, it did so on the same low note that Roker Park closed with. There have been many truly great days in the first two decades at the Stadium of Light, just as there will be many more in the decades to come. The final home game of the 20th season was the 400th league game to be staged at the stadium. Those games have seen many heroes in red and white - but none more so than the supporters in the stands who will be here for the next 400 and beyond.

PREMIER LEAGUE 2016-17

		HOME					AWAY						
P	W	D	L	F	A	W	D	L	F	A	Pts	Pos
38	3	5	11	16	34	3	1	15	12	35	24	20th

FA Cup: 3rd round, lost 0-2 in a replay at Burnley.

League Cup: 4th round, lost 0-1 at Southampton.

ATTENDANCES

Average (League): 41,172

Highest: 46,494 v Liverpool, 2 January 2017.

2016 17

SUNDERLAND A.F.C.

MATCH OF THE SEASON
Sunderland 2-1 Leicester City
Premier League · 3 December 2016

VICTOR ANICHEBE RUNS AT LEICESTER CITY'S WES MORGAN

DEFOE GETS THE SECOND GOAL

STADIUM OF LIGHT

131

SoL SURROUNDS

A trip to the Stadium of Light is more than just a visit to a football ground. Surrounding the stadium are numerous nods to the club's heritage along with ever improving facilities which complement the stadium area.

Starting on the south east corner you first reach from the city centre and working around the stadium finishing at the miner's lamp on the roundabout beside the club's administrative base, you will come across the following:

STADIUM **OF** LIGHT

132

STOKOE STATUE

Sculpted by Sean Hedges-Quinn, this bronze statue of Sunderland's 1973 FA Cup-winning manager Bob Stokoe, shows him in a moment from his celebratory run to Jim Montgomery at the final whistle of the cup final.

On the front of the plinth the inscription reads:

"The Manager The Man The 'Messiah' The Moment... 1973 FA Cup Final Winners Sunderland AFC v Leeds United 5th May 1973."

On the reverse of the plinth is a quote from Stokoe on the day before the famous final, "I didn't bring the magic. It's always been here... I just came back to find it." Bob Stokoe 4th May 1973. The statue was put in place following Stokoe's death in 2004.

HURLEY GATES

Sited at the Stadium of Light in November 2016, the 'Hurley Gates' aren't quite the Pearly Gates, but they came from the entrance to Sunderland's former training ground, The Charlie Hurley Centre. These are named after Sunderland's Player of the Century Charlie Hurley, who also has a suite named after him within the Stadium of Light. On the day the new position of the gates was revealed, Charlie was joined by his family and teammates from the 1964 promotion side he captained.

MURRAY GATES

Donated by former chairman Bob Murray, whose vision brought about the Stadium of Light, the Murray Gates bear the words 'For Us All' and 'Into the Light'. Unlike some chairmen who have wanted stadiums or stands named after them, Sir Bob simply left his mark by gifting these gates on either side of the stadium's main entrance.

FANS' STATUE

Pride of place outside the main entrance which is on the West Stand, Sunderland erected a statue, not to an individual, no matter how important the player, manager or chairman. Instead the club, which prides itself on its inclusiveness, gives pride of place to its supporters. The people who produced the world famous 'Roker Roar' now resident at the 'Stadium of Sound' are the people Sunderland AFC would cease to exist without. They are the people to whom the club ultimately belongs. Mirroring the words 'For Us All' on the Murray Gates, the Fans' Statue shows three generations and both genders in a bronze statue sculpted by Carl Payne, Andy Edwards and Julian Jeffrey.

133

GARDEN OF REMEMBRANCE

Ahead of a game with West Ham United in 2014 as part of the FA's commemorations of the centenary of the beginning of the First World War, a Garden of Remembrance was created around the Fans' Statue.

A small seated area accompanies a plaque listing the Sunderland players who gave their lives in both world wars. The Garden of Remembrance was opened by two military chaplains and SAFC chaplain, Father Marc Lynden-Smith.

LEITCH LATTICEWORK

A reminder that the Stadium of Light was a new chapter in the club's history. The two pieces 'Leitch latticework' in the West Stand car park are from the front of the main stand at Roker Park.

Both the Main Stand and the Clock Stand at Roker Park were designed by the famous football architect Archibald Leitch. His trade-mark was this 'criss-cross' latticework still in evidence at Everton, Portsmouth and Rangers.

MEN OF STEEL

Not actually something the football club have put in place, the figures you can see pushing boulders up the riverbank towards where the old Wearmouth Colliery pre-dated the Stadium of Light are part of the Sunderland Riverside Sculpture Trail. Produced by Graeme Hopper they are in tribute to the miners who worked below ground and were always wanting to come out of the darkness into the light.

PIT WHEEL

Just as the people who now live on the site of Roker Park appreciate that in years gone by, their homes are situated in a place where goals were currency, SAFC recognises that coal was the currency at the Stadium of Light before the footballers moved in.

First opened in 1826, more than half-a-century before the formation of the football club, the mine, first known as Pemberton Main Colliery and later Monkwearmouth Colliery, was - at 1,700 feet - the deepest coal mine in the world. A bright red model replica of pit-head winding gear is accompanied by a plaque paying tribute to the miners of Wearmouth.

BEACON OF LIGHT

The newest of the additions to the Stadium of Light surrounds, the Beacon of Light was still under construction as the stadium celebrated its 20th birthday.

Having started at Roker Park as a Football in the Community project the Foundation of Light is a charity that has grown out of the club. It uses the power of football to help people in the region and sometimes beyond. The Beacon of Light is a multi-functional centre of opportunity with over 6,000 people per week expected to use its four areas of education, health and well-being, sport and play and world of work.

AQUATIC CENTRE

Opened eleven years after the Stadium of Light, Sunderland Aquatic Centre is directly opposite the North Stand. The Olympic size swimming pool is the biggest between Leeds and Edinburgh and as well as regular swimming galas, has hosted international water-polo. The facility also houses a gym, sports-hall and exercise studio and although the Sunderland players have a swimming pool of their own at the Academy of Light, sometimes players recuperating from injury are to be found using the centre. Despite some of the diving in the modern game, there is no truth in the rumour that some players have used it as a warm up area.

HILTON GARDEN HOTEL

Opened in April 2016 after a 17-month construction period, the Hilton Garden Inn hotel is located so close to the Stadium of Light that it shares its car-park. With 141 rooms, a restaurant, bar and fitness centre it is the obvious place to stay for visitors to the SoL.

BLACK CAT HOUSE

The club's administrative hub. The main reception and ticket office are on the ground floor with officials' offices taking up the top two levels. Meeting rooms and corridors are decorated with iconic images of players throughout the club's history from George Holley to Niall Quinn. The club shop is located in the West Stand of the stadium, not at Black Cat House.

DAVY LAMP

4m tall, 1.5m wide and weighing 1.5 tonnes, the huge milled steel model of the miners' safety lamp, the Davy Lamp, was the brainchild of Fulwell sculptor Jim Roberts. Situated on a roundabout next to Black Cat House, as you approach the Stadium of Light, the Davy Lamp is permanently lit and was produced by Armitage Engineering of Washington.

STADIUM OF **Sound**

TAKE THAT

HARRY STYLES OF ONE DIRECTION

FOO FIGHTERS

From 2009 to 2016, the Stadium of Light became the Stadium of Sound as the world's top musical talent took to the stage as Sunderland's stadium transformed itself into one of the country's most elite venues for the biggest names in pop and rock.

On the very opening night of the stadium back in 1997, Status Quo showed what was possible when they landed on the pitch via helicopter and proceeded to blast out, 'Whatever You Want'. Quo weren't the first band to play the stadium though. They'd been beaten to it by 'Orange Orange, 'F.K.A. Upside Down', 'Clock' and 'Code Red' earlier the same evening.

In the early years of the Stadium of Light, pre-match bands on the pitch became a regular occurrence. Most notably for the final match of the record breaking 1998-99 campaign when 'Ready to Go' was the final part of the run out music, the band that made it a hit - 'Republica' - came to the Stadium of Light to perform the song that became synonymous with a golden early era at the ground.

Nonetheless, it took until 2009 for the stadium to seriously venture into the territory of being a stadium venue for the increasingly lucrative tours of the music industry. In 2009 there was no act bigger than 'Take That' who performed the opening two gigs at the Stadium of Light on 5 and 6 June as they opened their 'Circus' tour with an elaborately visual show that set the bar high.

Four days after Port Vale fan Robbie Williams left the stage, it was the turn of Manchester City followers 'Oasis' to provide an altogether different, but equally successful show. In a stadium renowned for its support, extensive support acts featured Kasabian, The Enemy and Reverend & the Makers.

P!nk performed in 2010, before Take That returned in 2011 to begin their Progress Live tour for four nights with support from the Pet Shop Boys. That summer also saw Kings of Leon headline, backed by Mona and White Lies.

2012 brought a self-indulgent and dull set from the Red Hot Chili Peppers that even disappointed many of their fans, before Coldplay produced what by common consent was one of the stadium's best gigs. Not everyone's cup of tea, Coldplay succeeded in having people raving about them despite playing in a deluge of heavy rain. Completing a hat-trick of big names in 2012, Bruce Springsteen & the E Street Band added to the variety of musical talent brought to the Stadium of Light with a show that predicted the arrival of Duncan Watmore two years later as 'the Boss' belted out a heartfelt 'Born to Run.'

A year later, Bon Jovi impressed with an outstanding show to a two thirds full stadium, before Rihanna broke stadium records by pulling in over 54,000 to her 'Diamonds' tour. Completing the line up in 2013 was a full day event billed as 'North East Live.' Like all concerts at the SoL, this demanded a lot of hard work behind the scenes by people at the club, but eventually was such a success that it was repeated a year later.

JLS, Amelia Lily, Conor Maynard, Lawson, Little Mix, Rita Ora, Stooshe, the Wanted and Union J made up the line-up in the initial North East Live. A year later Union J were part of the North East Live bill again, along with Jessie J, Jason Derulo, Rizzle Kicks, Rixton, Austin Mahone, Neon Jungle, Katy B, The Vamps and The Saturdays.

In 2014, the concerts at the SoL were all about one thing and that was One Direction, at the time the hottest act in the pop world. The arrival of One Direction brought another packed audience and immense attention to Sunderland, by now having overtaken Newcastle as the region's premier destination for the planet's biggest stars. Quite apart from the money brought into the local economy at hotels, restaurants and bars, one of the biggest things about the 19 major gigs in the 20 years of the stadium was that for a time the young people of Sunderland didn't have to troop off to Newcastle to see their pop favourites. Indeed the Tyneside public had to be grateful the Metro had finally come to Sunderland, so they could jump on it and come to Wearside for a good night out. For those old enough to remember David Bowie stepping onto the stage at Roker Park with the words, 'Hello Newcastle' this was a particular triumph.

When the Foo Fighters played at Sunderland in 2015, it was the second time they'd appeared on Wearside - having been headliners at the Radio One Big Weekend at Herrington Country Park on the weekend SAFC sealed promotion in 2005.

Last, but certainly not least, in the Stadium of Sound archive, Beyonce brought down the curtain on concerts for now in 2016. The American superstar's show was the opening night of the U.K. leg of her 'Formation' tour and like many of those which preceded it was a massive success.

One consequence of staging summer gigs though was the reduction of time for the ground-staff to work on the pitch during the close season. Subsequently Sunderland started seasons away from home and this became understood to be a contributory factor in Sunderland's costly slow starts to seasons. If the club can do better by getting early season points under their belts by beginning campaigns at home, every fan will be content to consign the era of stadium concerts to history. However, they were great while they lasted and possibly at some point in the future that will return. The main thing though is that Sunderland remembers that first and foremost it is a football club and football must come first.

Indeed one of the biggest names from the rock world to visit the Stadium of Light came for the football, Led Zeppelin front-man and Wolves director Robert Plant turning up for a match with his beloved Wanderers, while for the record, Family lead singer Roger Chapman also turned up to see Leicester.

COLDPLAY

BEYONCE

1997	Status Quo
2005	Republica
2009	Take That (2 nights) & Oasis
2010	Pink
2011	Take That (4 nights) & Kings of Leon
2012	Red Hot Chili Peppers, Coldplay and Bruce Springsteen and the E Street Band
2013	Bon Jovi, Rihanna & North East Live
2014	One Direction & North East Live
2015	Foo Fighters
2016	Beyonce

137

MARK NOBLE IN ACTION FOR ENGLAND U16 AGAINST GERMANY U16

ENGLAND U16 V BRAZIL U16

England have been regular visitors to the Stadium of Light during its opening two decades. Although Wembley Stadium didn't exist for the first quarter of a century after Roker Park was built, the national team only ever played three full internationals at Roker. Already that tally has been equalled at the Stadium of Light where the full England team have staged home matches in the nineties, the noughties and the 'teens.

Additionally, England have also hosted matches at U21, U20 and U16 level at the Stadium of Light, while at the U18 age group there has been an England Schools' international.

Four years after the stadium opened, it staged the final of the European U16 championships between Spain and France. One of the tournament's quarter-finals had also been played on Wearside, Spain playing Italy while the following year Spain played for a third time at U16 level. On that occasion they played Holland on the same day as the Stadium of Light played host to England against Germany.

Sadly, England's bids to host the FIFA World Cups of 2018 and 2006 failed. Sunderland had hosted three group games and a quarter-final when the World Cup came to England in 1966. Unfortunately, when England entertained the continent in Euro '96 Sunderland was not considered, as Roker Park was outdated and operating under a much reduced capacity from its heyday. Had the Stadium of Light been built a year earlier it's possible that - had plans been in place in time - Sunderland might have been used as one of the tournament stadia.

In contrast, when England bid to stage the 2006 FIFA World Cup, such was the status of the Stadium of Light as the biggest and best new stadium in the country, that it was earmarked as a potential semi-final venue. As the 20th anniversary of the Stadium of Light is celebrated in 2017, the Confederations Cup will have just been completed in Russia, serving as a 'warm-up to the World Cup' which will be held in Russia in 2018.

Despite much effort and an awful lot of resources that went into the bid for the 2018 World Cup to come to England, that bid was unsuccessful. Had FIFA decided to bring the World Cup back to the home of football for the first time in over half-a-century, then Sunderland had been accepted as a host city. As the twentieth anniversary of the Stadium of Light is celebrated the Wearside, the public would have been looking forward to seeing the world's top tournament.

That might be somewhat galling at the 2018 finals, when Wearside bars are packed with people cheering on England from afar. Quite possibly, there will be a Fan-zone set up in the city centre, as there has been for recent tournaments. It is regrettable that the boost, an influx of international football supporters would have given to Wearside, both financially and in terms of global profile, will not take place. That is not the fault of the club, or in any way a reflection of the Stadium of Light's ability to stage such fixtures - and remember the capacity would have been expanded further if the World Cup was to

KEVIN PHILLIPS CHALLENGES BELGIUM'S JACKY PEETERS

England 2-1 Belgium
10 October 1999, Friendly.

England U16 1-2 Brazil U16
16 July 2000, Friendly.

Spain U16 1-1 Italy U16
29 April 2001, European U16 Championship,
quarter-final. (Spain won 4-3 on penalties)

Spain U16 1-0 France U16
5 May 2001, European Championship final.

Holland U16 0-3 Spain U16
18 November 2002, International Tournament.

England U16 2-2 Germany U16
18 November 2002, International Tournament.

England U20 3-5 Italy U20
27 November 2002, Friendly.

England 2-0 Turkey
2 April 2003, Euro 2004 qualifying game.

England U21 2-0 Slovakia U21
10 June 2003, Euro Under 21 Championship
Group 7 qualifying game.

England Schools U18 0
Republic of Ireland Schools U18 1
18 April 2008, Centenary Shield.

Hetton Lyons CC 5-1 'Canada' (Liverpool)
29 April 2012, FA Carlsberg Sunday Cup final.

Cardinal Heenan 1-0 Bishop Challoner
8 May 2012, ESFA Premier League
U14 Schools Cup final.

England 2-1 Australia
27 May 2016, Friendly.

REPRESENTATIVE GAMES
AT THE
SoL

STADIUM OF LIGHT

STADIUM **OF** LIGHT

have come to Wearside. Perhaps one day England will get to host another major competition and if it does then SAFC will be at the forefront of clubs hoping to be involved.

England were most recently in action at the Stadium of Light when it was one of only two club grounds (along with Manchester City's Etihad Stadium) chosen alongside Wembley to stage warm-up games ahead of Euro 2016. Marcus Rashford began that game against Australia sensationally, with a goal after only two minutes as Roy Hodgson's side won 2-0, with Sunderland academy product Jordan Henderson in the side. As a packed Stadium of Light enjoyed the spectacle, little did anyone realise that the failure of the national side at the championships which followed would lead to Roy Hodgson departing, and Sunderland losing manager Sam Allardyce to the national team on the eve of what would subsequently prove to be a disastrous season.

Whereas Jermain Defoe was overlooked for England's game against Australia, on the first occasion England played at the Stadium of Light, Sunderland's Kevin Phillips was in the side - the fourth Sunderland player to represent England on Wearside. Perhaps forgotten now 'SuperKev' won the Sky Man of the Match award in that game for which Michael Gray made the squad, but not the team.

England won that encounter with Belgium 2-1, the winner being a spectacular strike from Jamie Redknapp after Belgium's Footballer of the Year Branko Stupar had equalised following Alan Shearer's opener. Shearer was one of two Newcastle players in the line-up along with sub Kieron Dyer. Putting partisanship to one side, the crowd afforded the Magpies wearing the Three Lions a reception so good that England coach - and ex-Magpie himself - Kevin Keegan commented, "The fans were terrific and never stopped trying to lift us. The reception for the two Newcastle players was fantastic and I'm really grateful for that."

While the visits of Belgium and Australia were friendly fixtures, England's visit in 2003 was for a key Euro 2004 Qualifying game with Turkey, who had been semi-finalists in the previous World Cup. Man of the Match on this occasion was a 17-year-old making his full debut, a certain Wayne Rooney. It was another superstar who scored the second goal with an injury-time penalty in a vital 2-0 win - David Beckham adding to a goal from Aston Villa's Darius Vassell. Rooney would get a goal for England at the Stadium of Light - but would have to wait until the Australia match in 2016.

Other than for full internationals, the Stadium of Light has welcomed England teams on five other occasions. The first was an U16 meeting with Brazil in millennium year, when a record crowd of 21,061 for an U16 international saw Brazil win 2-1 against a home team that featured Glen Johnson, still a Premier League performer in the 20th year of the Stadium of Light.

Two years later England were in U16 action on Wearside once again, this time with future Sunderland player Billy Jones in their side. Star names in the German team that day were Sami Khedira who would earn a World Cup winner's medal in 2014 and Kevin-Prince Boateng who went on to represent Ghana.

MARCUS RASHFORD SCORES ENGLAND'S FIRST V AUSTRALIA

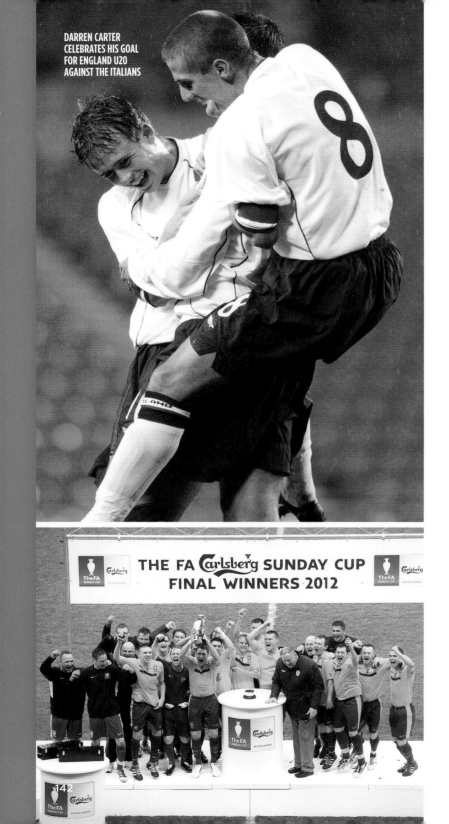

DARREN CARTER CELEBRATES HIS GOAL FOR ENGLAND U20 AGAINST THE ITALIANS

THE FA Carlsberg SUNDAY CUP FINAL WINNERS 2012

In an U16 double-header staged on the same day Holland would lose 3-0 to Spain who had Cesc Fabregas in their squad. In the previous year Spain had won the European U16 Championship by beating France 1-0 in the final at the Stadium of Light - the French including future Sunderland forward Anthony le Tallec. The Stadium of Light had also been a successful venue for Spain in a quarter-final they won on penalties after Fernando Torres had scored in a 1-1 draw with an Italy side that included Giorgio Chiellini. Also among the future stellar names in the squads that day was Andres Iniesta although he didn't play.

On the next two occasions England sides played at the Stadium of Light, by chance future Sunderland strikers appeared on the programme covers. Michael Chopra was the cover star at U20 level against Italy and netted twice. Joining him on the score sheet in a 3-5 defeat was future Sunderland midfielder Darren Carter, while other Sunderland connections in the team were Ben Clark and Calum Davenport.

Six-and-a-half months later, there was an upgrade to an U21 international and a similar upgrade in the future Sunderland man on the cover as Jermain Defoe lined up. On the bench that night was another future Sunderland forward in Darren Bent although he didn't come on. England's goals in a 2-0 win came from an own goal and one from Phil Jagielka, a man who David Moyes later tried to bring to the club.

Five years passed after the U21 game with Slovakia before another international took place at the Stadium of Light. The occasion was a schools U18 fixture with the Republic of Ireland who won with a first-half penalty scored by John Mulroy.

Schools internationals in the modern era lack the future stars you might once have seen in schools' games due to young players being tied to academies. However the England side did include Chris Smalling, later to play for Manchester United and England, but then of Chatham Grammar School. The game also marked the centenary of the Durham Schools' F.A.

Schools football brought another representative match to the Stadium of Light in 2012 in the shape of the ESFA Premier League U14 Schools Cup final. In the first game at the stadium to have fifth and sixth officials monitoring the goal-lines, Steven Gerrard's old school Cardinal Heenan defeated Bishop Challoner of the Hackney & Tower Hamlets SFA. The match was the second national cup final staged at the stadium in just over a week. Former SAFC Academy players Keith 'Rasher' Graydon, Robbie Clarkeson and Stephen Capper were in the Hetton Lyons squad who handsomely beat Merseyside team 'Canada.'

In the first 20 years at the Stadium of Light there have been eleven internationals, three of them full England games. The Republic of Ireland also played at the Stadium of Light against Sunderland just before the 2002 World Cup in a Benefit match for Niall Quinn. In the decades to come, hopefully many more prestigious matches will be staged at Sunderland.

Maybe even one day another major tournament will come to England and the Stadium of Light will be ready to welcome the world.

ENGLAND CAPTAIN DAVID BECKHAM SCORES FROM THE SPOT TO MAKE IT 2-0 AGAINST TURKEY

STADIUM OF LIGHT

SUNDERLAND A.F.C.

SoL Appearance and Goal Records 1997-2017

STATS CORRECT UP TO END OF 2016-17

MOST INDIVIDUAL APPEARANCES

NO	PLAYER	SAFC (INC SUB)		OTHER CLUBS	TOTAL
1	Michael Gray	125	1	Blackburn Rovers	126
2	Kevin Phillips*	117	1	Aston Villa	122
			1	WBA	
			1	England	
			2	Birmingham City	
3	John O'Shea	112	7	Manchester United	119
4	Darren Williams	112	1	Cardiff City	113
5	Thomas Sorensen	104	1	Aston Villa	107
			2	Stoke City	
6	Sebastian Larsson	103	1	Arsenal	106
			2	Birmingham City	
7	Niall Quinn	103			103
8	Phil Bardsley	100	1	Manchester United	102
			1	Stoke City	
9	Dean Whitehead	97	4	Stoke City	101
10	Lee Cattermole	99	1	Middlesbrough	100
11	George McCartney	97	2	West Ham United	99
12	Danny Collins	82	1	Chester City	84
			1	Stoke City	
13	Jody Craddock	80	1	Wolves	81
14	Julio Arca	79	1	Middlesbrough	80
15	Kieran Richardson	75	1	Fulham	76
16	Adam Johnson	71	3	Manchester City	74
17	Jack Colback	70	2	Newcastle United	72
18	Chris Makin	68	1	Ipswich Town	70
			1	Southampton	
19	Gavin McCann	65	1	Aston Villa	68
			2	Bolton Wanderers	
20	Daryl Murphy	66			66
21	Nyron Nosworthy	65			65
22	Kevin Kilbane*	57	2	WBA	64
			1	Everton	
			2	Wigan Athletic	
			2	Hull City	
23	Steed Malbranque	57	2	Fulham	59
24	Kenwyne Jones	53	3	Stoke City	58
			1	Southampton	
			1	Cardiff City	
25	Steven Fletcher	54	1	Burnley	57
			2	Wolves	
26	Simon Mignolet	50	4	Liverpool	54

* Players to have appeared for highest number of different teams (five). Kilbane and Quinn appearances for Ireland in Niall Quinn benefit match not included.

LEADING GOALSCORERS

NO	PLAYER	SAFC		OTHER CLUBS	TOTAL
1	Kevin Phillips	63	1	Aston Villa	64
2	Niall Quinn	33	0		33
3	Darren Bent	23	1	Ipswich Town	26
			2	Charlton Athletic	
4	Kenwyne Jones	18	0		18
	Marcus Stewart	17	1	Ipswich Town	18
	Jermain Defoe	17	1	Portsmouth	18
5	Julio Arca	14	0		14
6	Adam Johnson	12	1	Manchester City	13
7	Danny Dichio	12	0		12
8	Kevin Kyle	11	0		11
	Daryl Murphy	11	0		11
	Connor Wickham	9	2	Crystal Palace	11
9	Allan Johnston	10	0		10
	Stephen Elliott	10	0		10
	Dean Whitehead	10	0		10
	Stephane Sessegnon	10	0		10
	Fabio Borini	10	0		10
	Michael Bridges	9	1	Leeds United	10
10	Kieran Richardson	9	0		9
	Steven Fletcher	8	1	Wolves	9
11	Fraizer Campbell	8	0		8
	Craig Gardner	8	0		8
12	Lee Clark	7	0		7
	Gavin McCann	7	0		7
	Chris Brown	7	0		7
	David Connolly	7	0		7
	Asamoah Gyan	7	0		7
	Michael Chopra	4	1	Newcastle United	7
			2	Cardiff City	
13	Sebastian Larsson	6	0		6

LEADING OPPOSITION INDIVIDUAL GOALS

4	Gabby Agbonlahor	Aston Villa
4	Luis Suarez	Liverpool
4	Freddie Ljungberg	Arsenal
4	Sergio Aguero	Manchester City
4	Romelu Lukaku	1 WBA, 3 Everton
4	Christian Benteke	2 Villa, 1 Liverpool, 1 Crystal Palace
4	Cesc Fabregas	3 Arsenal, 1 Chelsea
4	James Milner	1 Leeds, 1 Newcastle, 2 Villa

SAFC HAT-TRICKS

Niall Quinn
Darren Bent
Jermain Defoe

VISITORS HAT-TRICKS

Freddie Ljungberg, Arsenal
Yannick Bolassie, Crystal Palace
Romelu Lukaku, Everton

MOST FREQUENT VISITORS

West Ham United 18, Arsenal 17, Chelsea 16, Everton 16.